CRIME AND THE FAMILY

Improving child-rearing and preventing delinquency

David Utting, Jon Bright and Clem Henricson

Occasional Paper 16

FAMILY POLICY STUDIES CENTRE

Published by

Family Policy Studies Centre
231 Baker Street
London NW1 6XE

Telephone 071 486 8211

ISBN 0 907051 65 0

June 1993

The **Family Policy Studies Centre** is an independent body which analyses family trends and the impact of policy. It is a centre of research and information. The Centre's Governing Council represents a wide spectrum of political opinion, as well as professional, academic, church, local authority and other interests.

This occasional paper, like all those in the series, represents the views of the authors and not necessarily those of the Family Policy Studies Centre.

Price: £12.95

Design and print by Intertype

Contents

Acknowledgements

We are especially grateful to Prof. David Farrington for guiding our early thoughts and identifying errors and omissions in the draft text; also to Erica De'Ath, Helen Edwards, Henri Giller, Gill Gorrell-Barnes, John Graham, Kathleen Kiernan, Peter Mortimore, Gillian Pugh and Ceridwen Roberts for reading the report at various stages.

They must take credit for many helpful suggestions and improvements, but cannot be held responsible for the interpretations or conclusions arrived at by the authors.

Thanks are also due to the following for their help in preparing the report: Betty Arnold, Louie Burghes, John Burns, Chris Butcher, John Carpenter, Lynn A.Curtis, Ioana Davies, Neil Dawson, Carolyn Douglas, East Moulsecoomb Playlink Project, Eileen Fendick, Christine Gaskell, Pauline Hardiker, Margaret Harrison, Bob Holman, Jane Ilsley, Josine Junger-Tas, Tim Kahn, Susan Kelly, Charles Keseru, Barry Knight, Helen Krarup, Legard Family Support Centre, Sue Lingard, Michael Little, Alison Maitland, Jane Mardon, Brenda McHugh, Sara Morrison, Annette Mountford, the National Children's Bureau Library, Newpin, Christopher Nuttall, Sarah O'Grady, Gerald R. Patterson and colleagues, Jacquie Pearson, John Rea Price, Lawrence J. Schweinhart and colleagues, Stephen Scott, Jean Taylor, Prof. Norman Tutt, John and Joyce Utting, Malcolm Wicks MP.

Special thanks go to Lucy Auty for typing the original draft and for proof-reading the final version.

The authors, the Family Policy Studies Centre, Crime Concern and NACRO would like to express their thanks to the General Electric Company plc.without whose generous financial support this report would not have been possible .

David Utting
Jon Bright
Clem Henricson
June 1993

4

Preface

Locked inside a classroom at Her Majesty's Young Offender Institution at Deerbolt, County Durham, an assorted group of burglars, car thieves and other convicted criminals earnestly debate the way they would handle a temper tantrum thrown by a toddler. Encouraged by their tutor, a consensus emerges that calm, collected reasoning offers a more effective approach than shouting or, worse still, lashing out at the child. As Rob, the 18-year old possesser of a string of burglary convictions, announces: "Slapping is all me Mum and Dad ever done to me, and look what happened."

The question of how best to discipline children is of more than passing interest to these 17 to 21-year olds. All of them are already fathers or about to become so – hence their decision to volunteer for classes in parent training. For ten weeks they are guided through the essentials of family planning, ante-natal care, birth and child development. They are taught the practicalities of nappy changing and potty training, home safety and entitlement to social security benefits. But they are also invited to consider the emotional challenges of raising a family.

Parent training courses are available to a very limited number of young men in Young Offender Institutions in England and Wales[1]. Their existence is, from one perspective, a matter of common sense: helping very young, inadequate fathers to play a more competent and responsible role. The greater an offender's sense of responsibility as a father, the lower the chances that he will find the time or inclination to persist in a life of crime.

Yet for all its potential advantages to those taking part, the target beneficiaries are really the offenders' children: babies and toddlers who may – if their parents know how to care for them – run a reduced danger of physical or sexual abuse and be less likely than their fathers to grow into teenage delinquents.

In that sense, parent training in prisons epitomises the practical value of an increasing fund of knowledge that exists about the links between families, upbringing and criminal behaviour. It
makes explicit an understanding that the way, as well as the conditions, in which parents raise children from an early age exerts a powerful influence over their risks of future criminality. It offers hope that the cycle of criminal and abusive parents rearing criminal and abusive children can be broken.

The connections between delinquency and the family and their potential to form the basis for a programme of social crime prevention are the subject of this report.

Structure of this Report

Chapter 1 sets the scene with an introduction to the main sources of research, features of which are discussed in greater detail in Chapter 2.

Based on the available evidence, Chapters 3, 4 and 5 explore the scope for crime prevention initiatives based on support for families themselves, on ways that schools and families can work together to reduce the risks of delinquency and how families and community organisations can do the same.

After a review of relevant legislation, including the 1989 Children Act and the 1991 Criminal Justice Act in Chapter 6, the report concludes with a presentation of policy options and recommendations.

[1] Caddle, D. (1991)

Introduction

"We wish that people did not behave in ways that are socially troublesome, and we would like to know why they do and what can best be done to stop them"
Barbara Wootton[1]

Every so often, social surveys ask people who they think is to blame for juvenile crime. The answer by large majorities over the past 25 years has invariably been "the parents". The British public would doubtless sympathise with the stone mason who inscribed an ancient Mesopotamian tablet with a lament that the world would degenerate *"because children no longer obeyed their parents"*.[2]

The inability of successive governments in modern Britain to control a tide of rising crime – whether measured by police records[3] or the much larger figures revealed by random surveys of the population at large[4] – has done little to shake popular belief that responsibility lies with individuals.[5]

There is, in fact, compelling statistical evidence that connects changes in the crime rate with trends in economic consumption. Home Office research demonstrates how property offences grow faster from year to year when the rate of increase in personal spending slows down, yet crimes of violence speed up as soon as people go out and start spending more money.[6] The same study suggests that when the number of young men in the population goes up in the aftermath of a baby boom, there is a corresponding rise in most types of crime.

Such attempts to chart the big picture suggest that there are social and economic pressures that make it more (or less) likely that individuals will commit those acts of anti-social behaviour that are officially outlawed as "crime". But they cannot answer the specific question, *"Why do they do it?"* which Barbara Wootton posed more than 30 years ago in a pioneering review of the, then, available research into the roots of criminality.[7] As two contemporary searchers for the causes of crime, the Harvard criminologist James Q. Wilson and his psychologist colleague Richard J. Herrnstein, note, the baby boom may help explain why crime rose in the 1960s and 1970s, but it cannot tell us why some "baby boomers" became criminals and others did not.[8]

Rising crime

For the past quarter of a century, recorded crime figures in England and Wales have risen, on average, by around 5 per cent per year.[9] Thus, while 1.6 million offences were recorded by police in 1970 (and 2.5 million in 1980) the total for 1992 reached 5.6 million[10] (**Table 1**). Around 600,000 equivalent offences were recorded by police in Scotland.[11] All but 5 per cent of recorded offences were non-violent crimes involving property (**Table 2**). Criminal activity on an altogether greater scale is uncovered, however, by the 1992 British Crime Survey, conducted in more than 10,000 English and Welsh homes, which projects a total of 15 million crimes a year, the majority of which were never even reported to the police.[12]

Inspection of records from police forces and the courts suggests that crime is commonly committed by young men. Over 80 per cent of known offenders are male; almost half (46 per cent) are aged under 21, and one in five are under 17. The age at which males are most likely to be convicted or cautioned for an offence is 15 to 18 and the comparable "peak" age for female offending is 15[13] (**Table 3**).

Even judged by the minority of crimes which are ever "solved", law-breaking among young people is a common occurrence. A Home Office analysis of criminal records for a random sample of those born in 1953 found that one in three men, but only 8% of women, had been convicted of crimes on a "standard list" of offences[14] by the age of 35[15] (**Table 4**).

Perhaps surprisingly to anyone unaware of changes in the juvenile justice system, the number of known young offenders fell during the 1980s. Measured per head of the total population aged 10 to 16, the numbers found guilty or cautioned for "indictable" offences[16] dropped by 17 per cent between 1981 and 1991[17] (**Table 5**). Demography in the shape of a 25 per cent drop in the overall juvenile population offers a partial explanation, but more significant has been a successful national effort to reduce the number of juveniles taken to court, especially those aged 14 and under. There is a shortage of hard evidence as to true changes in the incidence of juvenile offending, but there are indications that the apparent decline of recent years is, in the words of the Cambridge criminologist, David Farrington, *"an illusion caused by changes in police policies"*.[18] Certainly, the Home Office,[19] backed by the Association of Chief Police Officers (ACPO) and Superintendants' Association,[20] takes the view that the number of informal, unrecorded warnings given to young people by police has risen markedly. This may have reduced the extent to which some juvenile offences[21] are reported to police at a time when detection rates have, in any case, been in decline. As a result, it is argued that offending rates per head of the juvenile population may have increased during the 1980s by as much as 54 per cent.[22] The known offending rate among young people aged over 17 but under 21 has, meanwhile, risen by 13 per cent.[23]

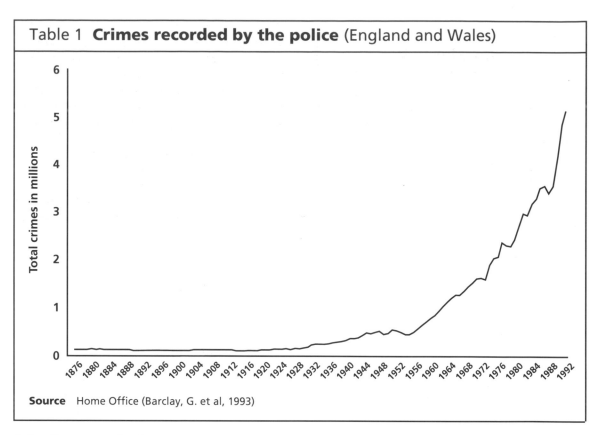

Table 1 **Crimes recorded by the police** (England and Wales)

Total crimes in millions (y-axis, 0 to 6)

x-axis years: 1876, 1880, 1884, 1888, 1892, 1896, 1900, 1904, 1908, 1912, 1916, 1920, 1924, 1928, 1932, 1936, 1940, 1944, 1948, 1952, 1956, 1960, 1964, 1968, 1972, 1976, 1980, 1984, 1988, 1992

Source Home Office (Barclay, G. et al, 1993)

A family connection?

The crime wave represents one of the more dramatic social trends of the past 30 years. It was, therefore, only to be expected that suspicion, amidst attempts to explain its unwelcome rise, would fall on other major social changes that have left their mark on late 20th century Britain. Notable among these are trends affecting the family.[24]

A seven-fold increase in the divorce rate over the past 30 years has created speculation that young criminals could be the products of a growing number of "broken homes". A rapid rise in the proportion of mothers with dependent children who go out to work has led to theorising that dual-earner families could be leaving children free to roam the streets outside school hours, with mischievous consequences. Likewise, a rapid growth in the

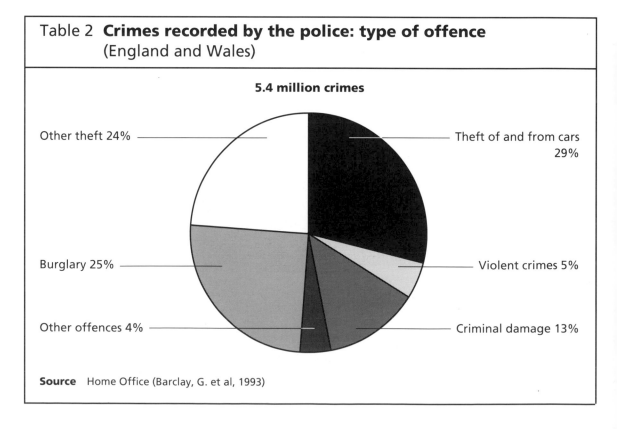

Table 2 **Crimes recorded by the police: type of offence** (England and Wales)

5.4 million crimes

- Other theft 24%
- Theft of and from cars 29%
- Burglary 25%
- Violent crimes 5%
- Other offences 4%
- Criminal damage 13%

Source Home Office (Barclay, G. et al, 1993)

8

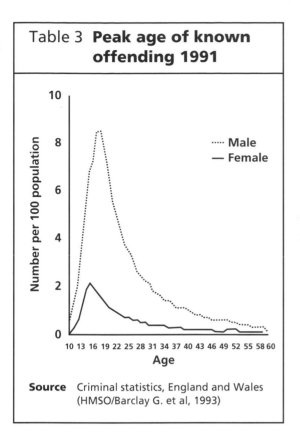

Table 3 Peak age of known offending 1991

Number per 100 population

····· Male
— Female

Age

Source Criminal statistics, England and Wales
(HMSO/Barclay G. et al, 1993)

The task of sifting the evidence for these and other assertions has been taken up by academic researchers in "western" societies around the world. When the era of rapid family change had barely begun, Barbara Wootton drew on studies dating back to before the Second World War to consider the evidence. Family poverty and educational failure were among the headline factors which she discovered had been linked to later delinquency.[25] Since then, work from the diverse standpoints of sociology, psychiatry, psychology and the umbrella discipline of criminology has proliferated. The modern reviewer can refer to detailed studies conducted in, among other countries, Canada, New Zealand, Finland, Sweden and the Netherlands as well as a substantial body of research in Great Britain and the United States. One recent paper, analysing the impact of broken homes on delinquency, was able to draw on 50 relevant, English-language studies.[26]

Problems and pitfalls

There can be no pretence that results from so considerable a volume of research work are in complete accord. While unravelling the internal dynamics and external pressures affecting families, the investigator walks through a methodological minefield. Comparisons between the many studies of delinquency are dogged by such fundamental concerns as the definition of criminal behaviour and the way it should be measured. For

number of lone parent families – from one in sixteen in 1961 to almost one in five today – has produced claims that children with only one parent supervising them must run a greater risk of delinquency.

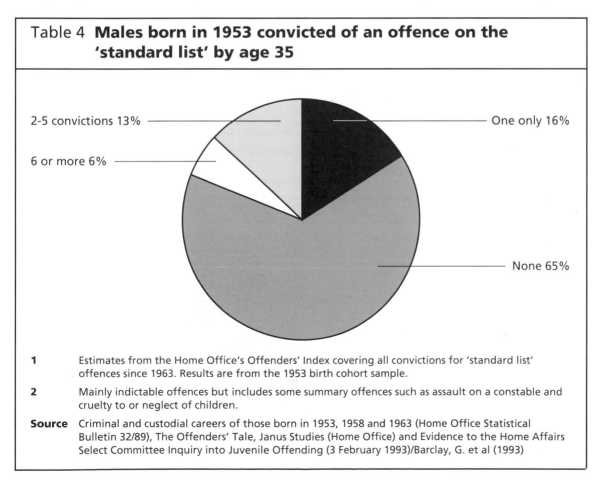

Table 4 Males born in 1953 convicted of an offence on the 'standard list' by age 35

2-5 convictions 13%

6 or more 6%

One only 16%

None 65%

1   Estimates from the Home Office's Offenders' Index covering all convictions for 'standard list' offences since 1963. Results are from the 1953 birth cohort sample.

2   Mainly indictable offences but includes some summary offences such as assault on a constable and cruelty to or neglect of children.

Source Criminal and custodial careers of those born in 1953, 1958 and 1963 (Home Office Statistical Bulletin 32/89), The Offenders' Tale, Janus Studies (Home Office) and Evidence to the Home Affairs Select Committee Inquiry into Juvenile Offending (3 February 1993)/Barclay, G. et al (1993)

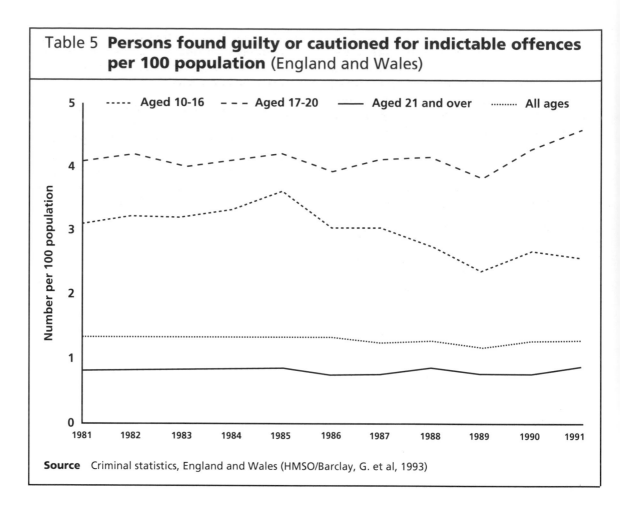

Table 5 Persons found guilty or cautioned for indictable offences per 100 population (England and Wales)

Legend: ----- Aged 10-16 - - - Aged 17-20 —— Aged 21 and over ·········· All ages

Y-axis: Number per 100 population (0 to 5)

X-axis: 1981 1982 1983 1984 1985 1986 1987 1988 1989 1990 1991

Source Criminal statistics, England and Wales (HMSO/Barclay, G. et al, 1993)

example, a delinquency study focusing on "official" records – convictions in the courts and formal cautioning by police – is apt to produce a different picture from research where teenagers themselves are asked to "self-report" their criminal activities. The results from a survey which defines delinquency as offenders with one or more criminal convictions may sit awkwardly alongside studies where "delinquency" is taken to include truancy from school, swearing in the street, or under-age drinking in pubs. Asking teachers to rate the behaviour of children in their class can, likewise, produce a very different assessment of just who is "anti-social" than a survey which depends on asking their parents.[27]

One cautionary tale is provided by some of the earliest and most extensive studies in the United States, published by Sheldon and Eleanor Glueck.[28] Their painstaking 10 and 15 year follow-up comparisons between the circumstances of 500 boys imprisoned in correctional facilities and a matched sample of 500 non-delinquent boys from comparable backgrounds in Boston cast light on the importance of the relationship between parents and children, including styles of supervision and discipline in the home. Yet failings in the design of the research – such as the use of interviewers who were told beforehand which families included a delinquent boy – mean many of the findings have, for many years, been treated with suspicion.[29]

Interpretative difficulties can also arise when attempts are made to compare results from methodologically different sources. The tendency for some investigators to angle their research in support or confutation of the explanatory theories and underlying ideologies which abound in criminology is another potential source of confusion for policy makers wanting to tease out practical advice.[30]

Fortunately, it is not unusual for different approaches to the same issue – a study of teenagers and their families using "official" records of theft convictions, say, and a "self-report" survey of stealing – to arrive at the same, or similar, conclusions. This review has found that the available research tells enough of the same story about crime and the family for sensible conclusions about the potential for preventing delinquency to be drawn.

Setting the scene

Longitudinal surveys, where children's progress is monitored from an early age, make it possible to observe how their behaviour patterns and family circumstances change as they grow older. Since a number of these prospective studies have been conducted in Britain, they provide a useful introduction to what is known on both sides of the Atlantic about crime and the family. What follows here is an outline of three of the best-constructed and most informative surveys. The aim, at this stage, is to describe the headline findings; some of the results are subject to more detailed consideration under various headings in Chapter 2.

1 The National Survey of Health and Development (The 1946 Cohort Study)

This was an investigation into the health, growth and development of over 5,300 children born in March 1946 which took *"a unique opportunity to study law-breakers"*. Criminal records were obtained for English and Welsh children in the survey from the age of 8.

Reported by Michael Wadsworth in 1979 the results show that 17.9 per cent of the boys and 2.5 per cent of the girls had been found guilty by a court or formally cautioned by police before their 21st birthday.[31] A "Social Acceptability of Crime" (SAC) scale was devised to distinguish between victimless offences, like speeding, and more serious crimes, like burglary and acts of violence. It allowed Wadsworth to demonstrate that boys who had committed two or more offences – described as "recidivists" – tended to be involved in more serious crime than others who came to the attention of the police.

His other main findings were that:

- Delinquency as indicated by criminal records was three times more common among the sons of unskilled manual workers than those of professional and salaried workers. A specially-devised measure of "social group", taking account of parents' educational background, showed that serious offending was more common among the sons of manual workers.

- Four out of ten male recidivists (with two or more convictions) came from large families with three or more brothers and sisters. This represented a significantly greater risk of delinquency than found among children in smaller families – yet three quarters of children in large families did not become recidivists.

- Having a mother who had worked when they were aged 0 to 6 failed to distinguish boy delinquents from non-delinquents, once factors like socio-economic status and overcrowding at home were taken into account.

- Broken homes were related to delinquency, with the earliest breaks (aged 0 to 4) linked to the least acceptable offending when children grew older.

- Delinquent girls, although relatively few in number, were almost twice as likely to come from a home broken by divorce, separation or bereavement as boys.

- Teachers' assessments of boys' attitudes to work and conduct at age 10 were of some significance in identifying later offenders, but 79 per cent of children rated "poor" or "lazy" did not acquire a criminal record. Ratings by teachers suggesting a lack of parental interest in their children's education were also correlated with future delinquency.[32]

2 The Newcastle 1,000 Family Study

The survey began by investigating the health of children born in Newcastle upon Tyne during May and June, 1947. The study was resumed in 1979, and included a comparison between the backgrounds of children who later acquired a criminal record and those who did not.[33]

Professor Israel Kolvin and his colleagues devised six indices which, collectively, pointed to family deprivation. These were: *marital disruption; parental illness; poor domestic care of the child and home; dependence on social services; overcrowding and poor mothering*. Families subject to three or more of these factors were described in the report as *"multiply deprived"*.

The researchers compared their data on deprivation with later, official crime records. The aim was to identify factors which appeared to have protected some severely deprived children against delinquency and other factors which seemed to have made even children who were not socially deprived more vulnerable to later law-breaking:

- By the age of 33, one in four men and one in twenty women had committed offences. Of the children who were found guilty or cautioned before the age of 15, three out of four had gone on to commit later offences.

- One in six children living in more affluent districts became delinquent compared to one in three in the poorest neighbourhoods.

- Delinquency was strongly correlated with deprivation. Six out of ten boys (and 9 per cent of girls) who came from "multiply-deprived" backgrounds acquired a criminal record.

- Seven out of ten deprived children receiving poor maternal and domestic care before the age of 5 became delinquent compared with four out of ten whose parental care was judged to be good.

- Those children from deprived backgrounds who avoided a criminal record had tended to enjoy good parental care and supervision in a less crowded home. Approaching puberty, they showed relatively good intellectual development and a positive temperament.

- Children who became delinquent from homes which had not been classified as deprived were more likely to have experienced emotional stress and, in some cases, to have been raised by an unmarried, relatively young mother. By the age of 10 or 11, they tended to show low levels of intelligence and educational achievement, as well as behavioural difficulties.

- In adolescence, a "positive" temperament and educational progress continued to be identifiable characteristics of socially deprived teenagers who kept out of trouble. Family contact with the school and, in girls, the continued presence of their natural father at home, also emerged as "protective" factors.

- Teenagers from non-deprived backgrounds who became criminally involved took noticeably less part in shared, family activities. Their parents maintained less contact with school and were more likely to have been classified by the researchers as "ineffective personalities".

3 The Cambridge Study in Delinquent Development

Pursuing the fortunes of over 400 working-class boys in South London, mostly born during 1953, this survey is one of the most detailed criminological investigations ever undertaken. Its principal aims were to discover how far criminality could be predicted, why delinquency began and to explain why most teenage delinquents – but not all – ceased their criminal activities on reaching their 20s.

Boys were interviewed and tested in their schools by psychologists at ages 8, 10 and 14. Their intelligence, achievement, personality and psychomotor skills were assessed. Teachers completed questionnaires about the boys' attainment and behaviour in school and, while still at primary school, the researchers questioned classmates about the boys' popularity, daring, dishonesty and troublesomeness. Parents were also interviewed annually by social workers until the boys were aged 14-15. Information was collected about their incomes, living conditions, family circumstances and child-rearing practices.

Details of convictions for all but the most minor offences were gathered. The boys, themselves, were also asked to give a self-report account of any offending. They were surveyed beyond the school-leaving age when they were 16, 18, 21, 25 and 32.

In 1986, the year of the most recent interviews, the researchers were in touch with 94 per cent of the original sample.[34]

- One in five boys were convicted as juveniles and one in three by the age of 25. Fewer than 6 per cent of the sample accounted for half the total number of officially recorded convictions by age 32.

- Men convicted at the earliest ages tended to become the most persistent offenders. Out of 22 chronic offenders who had been convicted of nine or more offences by age 32, all had appeared before a juvenile court before their 15th birthday.

- Many young delinquents, especially those convicted only once or twice, had no convictions after the age of 19 or 20. But about half those convicted between the ages of 10 and 20 were reconvicted between the ages of 21 and 32.[35]

- Marriage, girlfriends and the reduced influence of delinquent friends were most often mentioned as reasons for ceasing criminal activities. But young offenders who married women with criminal convictions continued to offend at the same rate as before.

- Delinquents tended to be those who had been identified as impulsive, aggressive, troublesome, unpopular and dishonest at primary school. Their intelligence and attainment scores were lower than average.

- Neither the father's occupational status, nor having a mother who worked were related to later delinquency. But future offenders were more likely to have: been part of low income and larger families; lived in run-down housing; received help from the social services and shown signs of physical neglect by their parents.

- Experience of divorce or parental separation before the age of 10 was associated with future delinquency, as was conflict between parents in the home.

- Parents whose child-rearing practices included harsh or erratic discipline, a cruel, passive or neglecting attitude and poor overall supervision were more likely to produce delinquent teenagers.

- Children were more likely to grow into delinquency if one or both parents had a background of offending or if they had an older sibling who was delinquent.

Donald West and David Farrington, co-authors of the Cambridge study, found one of the best predictors of later delinquency was the rating of boys' troublesomeness at age 8-10 by teachers and class-

Table 6	Percentages of self-reported and official delinquents among boys in the Cambridge Study in Delinquent Development who displayed various adverse features		
Adverse features	84 youths with official record of juvenile offences	80 self-reported delinquents (defined by tests at ages 14 and 16)	83 delinquents defined by combined measure
'Troublesome' at primary school	44.6	34.1	47.3
Low family income	33.3	28.0	33.3
Large family size	32.3	27.3	31.3
Criminal parent	37.9	34.0	35.0
Unsatisfactory child-rearing	32.3	28.4	31.6
Lowest quartile of IQ	31.1	28.4	31.4
Source West, D.J. (1982)			

mates[36] (**Table 6**). But they identified four other, independently important, predictors of offending. These were:

1) *economic deprivation*

2) *family criminality*

3) *parental mishandling*

4) *school failure*

Coming from a large family emerged as a significant precursor of delinquency, but essentially because such families also tended to be poor and inadequately housed. Coming from a low income family, a large family or having a parent with a criminal record effectively doubled the risk of later delinquency. The same was true of boys who had below average IQs or who suffered from "unsatisfactory" parenting, as assessed by social workers (**Table 6**). Of the 63 boys in the study who combined **three or more** of these factors during their primary school years, almost half became delinquent as juveniles.

Further evidence

From this glance at the core of longitudinal research conducted in Britain it is already apparent that the tangled roots of delinquency lie, to a considerable extent, inside the family. Children whose families suffer financial and environmental poverty are clearly at greater risk than those whose parents have the income to provide them with a comfortable, uncrowded home. Yet, as the authors of the Newcastle study observed, social deprivation does not appear sufficient **on its own** for delinquency to develop.[37] Factors within the care-giving environment (and, possibly, in the children

themselves) are seen to modify the influence of poverty and disadvantage. A comparable point was made by Michael Rutter and Henri Giller in their exhaustive review of the literature on juvenile delinquency.[38] Noting that any statistical relationship between social status and delinquency in the Cambridge study disappeared once the influence of poor parental supervision was taken into account,[39] they concluded that:

"The indicators are that most of the modest association between social class and delinquency is probably due to the parental and family problems sometimes associated with low social status, rather than low social status per se."[40]

Two further studies in the United Kingdom have examined the question of parental supervision in some detail. Harriett Wilson pursued the relationship between a strict parenting regime and absence of delinquency which she had first observed among families living in deprived inner city areas of the West Midlands.[41] Her survey focused on two samples of large families including a 10 or 11-year old boy and at least one older brother.[42] One group were chosen from high crime, inner city neighbourhoods and the other lived on run-down suburban estates. None of the parents had been educated beyond secondary school, and the two samples of 60 families reflected a comparable range of deprivation. "Social handicap" was scored by combinations of father's social class, family size, adequacy of the boys' school clothing, school attendance records and parental contact with the school.

Mothers were asked about their degree of supervision, including the extent to which their 10 to 11-year olds were allowed to roam the streets and

13

their knowledge of their children's whereabouts. The children were also interviewed about misbehaviour ranging from nuisance activities to more serious offences like shoplifting and burglary.

Checking the criminal records of all 595 children aged 10 to 17 in the survey, it emerged that delinquency rates were higher in the inner city, but not to a significant degree. What was distinctive was the discovery that the rate of delinquency in those families classified as most severely socially handicapped was nearly three times that of families whose degree of social disadvantage was relatively low. Delinquency was almost twice as common in homes where one of the parents had a criminal record. Yet even those correlations were modest compared with the discovery that the rate of delinquency in homes where parental supervision was lax was more than seven times that for families assessed as being strict.

Wilson carried out a follow-up survey six years later when the proportion of households with one or more delinquent sons had increased markedly.[43] She found no reason to alter her central conclusion that parental supervision was the most important single factor in determining juvenile delinquency and that social disadvantage is probably more important than parental criminality. In her later study she characterised the family influences at work like this:

> "Large family size and overcrowding lead to unsupervised play in streets and yards, and early severance of mother-child contact affects behavioural training. Children learn to adapt by developing techniques of aggression and withdrawal ... Lax supervision in this setting is not a deliberate choice of a permissive style of parenting: it carries an element of abandonment."[44]

Among the concurring evidence, a survey in Liverpool found that 11 to 15 year old boys who were left free on the streets for three or more hours an evening were markedly more prone to engage in vandalism.[45] A more recent study of 72 families in high-crime areas of Glasgow suggested that the "traditional child-rearing pattern of strict, working-class parents" appeared to offer children protection against later delinquency.[46]

Qualifications to this picture are introduced – although not unhelpfully – by the work of David Riley and Margaret Shaw, two Home Office researchers, who used interviews with 750 teenagers and their mothers to test the links between parental supervision and delinquent behaviour.[47] The study made use of a national rather than a specially "high risk" sample of families, and focused on 14 and 15 year olds – girls and boys who were already

close to the peak age for offending.

Like other "self-report" surveys, the results suggested a level of law-breaking well beyond anything recorded in the official statistics. Some 49 per cent of the boys and as many as 39 per cent of girls claimed to have committed one or more illegal acts in the previous year. There is, however, reason to suspect that girls are generally inclined to overstate any offending behaviour by comparison with boys in such surveys.[48] It is also important to note that the crimes most commonly admitted were among the least serious: smashing bottles in the street, fare-dodging and deliberately damaging school property, followed by low-value shoplifting, spray-painting walls and stealing within the family.[49]

Applying a less strict definition of "parental supervision" than Harriett Wilson (but one which was considered more appropriate to adolescent lifestyles) mothers were asked how often they knew whom their son or daughter was with, where they were going and what they were doing.

- **Girls** who broke the law appeared, in particular, to suffer from a range of communication difficulties with their parents.

- **Boys** were found to be less well supervised than girls and delinquency was less common among teenagers whose parents kept a check on their various activities.

There were, however, other factors in this age group that were more closely related to delinquency than parental supervision. Boys who reported having friends who committed criminal offences were nearly eight times more likely to be delinquent themselves. Thus, if boys associated with a delinquent peer group, it made no difference to their own behaviour whether their activities appeared to be well or poorly monitored by their parents.

The altered definition of parental supervision may partially explain why its primacy in Wilson's study was supplanted by the question of whether teenage boys were involved with a delinquent peer group. But so, too, may the difference in age between the children being observed. The "focus" boys in Wilson's survey were four years younger than those in Riley and Shaw. This points to a common sense explanation that the amount of parental supervision that pre-teen children receive may well be strongly related to their later behaviour, but that the influence of parents diminishes as they grow older and the influence of their peers increases. Those who have been least well-supervised by their parents when young and who have achieved least in primary school are more likely to

14

mix with "the wrong crowd" of other anti-social children. In other words, the power of parents in a crime prevention context is at its greatest before their children reach the age of 10.

According to Prof. Israel Kolvin and his colleagues who conducted the Newcastle 1000 Survey: "Good parenting protects against the acquisition of a criminal record."[50] Consideration of any practical applications for this knowledge in terms of crime prevention needs, however, to be preceded by a careful examination of the various family factors that appear most likely to be implicated. A more detailed breakdown and discussion of the evidence is undertaken in the next chapter.

1 Wootton, B. (1959)

2 Cited in Junger-Tas, J (1993)

3 Home Office Research and Statistics (1993)

4 Mayhew, P.& Aye Maung, N. (1992)

5 For example, Banks et al.(1975) and Mori Poll for Home Office (1989)

6 Field, S. (1990)

7 Wootton, B. (1959)

8 Wilson, J.Q. & Herrnstein, R.J.(1985)

9 Barclay, G.C.(1993)

10 ibid and Home Office Research and Statistics Department Bulletin 9/93 (April 1993)

11 In 1992 Scottish police recorded 590,000 "crimes" and 434,000 "offences" - a definition covering lesser assaults, acts of vandalism and motoring offences. See Scottish Office (1993)

12 Mayhew, P. & Aye Maung, N. (1992)

13 Barclay, G.C. et al (1993)

14 Motoring offences, drunkenness and other minor offences were not included

15 Home Office Statistical Department (1989)

16 Charges which, if prosecuted, entitle the defendant to trial by jury

17 Barclay, G.C. et al (1993)

18 Farrington, D.P.(1992)

19 ibid.

20 Association of Chief Police Officers of England, Wales and Northern Ireland / the Police Superintendants Association (1993)

21 Notably shoplifting. ibid.

22 ibid.

23 ibid. Note, however, that this age group includes the tail-end of the 1960s "baby boom".

24 For an overview of family trends, see Kiernan and Wicks (1990) The definition of "family" used there, and in this report, is a broad one of dependent children and one or both parents.

25 Wootton, B. (1959)

26 Wells, L.E. & Rankin, J.H. (1991)

27 See Rutter, M.et al.(1970).

28 Glueck, S. & Glueck, E.T. (1950)

29 See Laub, J.H. & Sampson, R.J.(1988) for an attempt to salvage useful data and conclusions from the research.

30 For a helpful summary of the various theories, see Rutter and Giller (1983)

31 Wadsworth (1979). The figures quoted were adjusted to take account of sampling bias

32 See Rutter, M.et al (1970) for description of the dangers of relying on teacher or parental assessments as "indicators" of delinquency potential

33 Kolvin, I. et al (1990)

34 The Cambridge Study has led to the publication of numerous books and papers. The main findings and interpretation can be found in: West, D.J. (1969); West, D.J. & Farrington, D.P. (1973); West, D.J. & Farrington, D.P. (1977); West, D.J. (1982) and Farrington, D.P. & West, D.J. (1990).

35 65 re-convicted out of 124 convicted under the age of 20

36 Problems with teacher assessments are discussed in Rutter, M.; Tizard, J. and Whitmore, K. (1970), see also Graham, J. (1989)

37 Kolvin, I. et al (1990)

38 Rutter, M. & Giller, H. (1983)

39 Farrington, D.P. (1979)

40 Rutter, M. & Giller, H. (1983)

41 Wilson (1975)

42 Wilson, H. (1980)

43 From 38 per cent to 59 per cent. Wilson, H.(1987)

44 ibid.

45 Gladstone, F. (1978)

46 Layborn, A. (1986)

47 Riley, D. & Shaw, M. (1985)

48 See Wilson, J.Q. and Herrnstein, R.J. (1985) for a description of this phenomenon

49 The researchers also draw attention to the 73% response rate from their survey sample. It is possible that families whose children were most involved in delinquency refused to take part and that trivial offences were over-represented as a result.

50 Kolvin, I. et al (1990)

CHAPTER 2

Delinquent families: myth and reality

"The human infant has no sense of 'right' dress, safe driving speeds, moral sex behaviour, private property or any of the other norms of society, whether custom or law. Conformity, not deviation, must be learned." F Ivan Nye[1]

How early can anyone tell if a child is at risk of growing into a criminal? Boys in the Cambridge Study in Delinquent Development were aged 8 to 10, when relevant factors like their aggression, educational difficulties and family background were first observed.[2] For example, nearly half those identified as "troublesome" at primary school later became delinquent (See **Table 6** in previous chapter). Among the Newcastle cohort, as many as 70 per cent of children assessed before the age of 5 as *"deprived and receiving poor domestic care"* were eventually convicted of a criminal offence.[3] A cohort study of New Zealand children born in 1972-3 found that pre-school behaviour problems were the single best predictor of anti-social disorders in 11 year olds and delinquency by age 15.[4]

Aggressive behaviour in primary school children has, in turn, been linked by studies in Britain and America to harsh early upbringing provided by hostile, abusive or punitive treatment by parents.[5] Parental conflict, a disruptive home life and high levels of family stress provide more pieces of the jigsaw.[6] Studies in Sweden and Britain attest further to the durability of aggression in anti-social children as they grow towards adolescence.[7]

Research conducted at the University of Minnesota takes the time-frame on aggression back as far as infancy, relating it (and other conduct problems in 4 and 5 year olds) to a deficient relationship with their mothers[8] observed as early as age 12 or 18 months.[9] Insecure boys who lacked warm, sharing relationships with their parents and who were judged to be receiving inadequate or hostile care were specially likely to be rated aggressive by their pre-school teachers.

This mosaic of information on the behavioural characteristics of children in different age groups suggests that the origins of delinquency and criminality can sometimes be traced back to the cradle itself. But then the theories developed by the psychiatrist John Bowlby on the adverse consequences when mothers fail to "bond" with their babies have been in circulation for more than 40 years.[10] In his view, infants whose emotional needs have been neglected are liable to respond to their comfortless and unpredictable treatment by becoming withdrawn, or else unsociably aggressive. By contrast, the child who has formed a warm, secure attachment with its parent(s) has a positive model of the adult world, helping it to grow up with self-esteem, self-confidence and respect for others. Bowlby compared the importance of a baby receiving maternal affection to *"the role of vitamins in physical health."*

One early-stated conclusion of this report is that the scope for family-based crime prevention work begins as early as parenthood itself. To frame proposals of this type is not, however, to imply that particular babies, without intervention, are predestined to an anti-social or criminal lifestyle. Nor is it recommended that individual infants and families should – or even could – be singled-out and labelled as potentially delinquent. Each developmental phase of a young child's life sets the stage for the way that she or he will adapt to the next series of developmental tasks.[11] It is plainly nonsense to suppose that every child who suffers a troubled infancy will be pitched into a disturbed adolescence or that once placid toddlers never grow into delinquents. One of the most telling criticisms made of Bowlby's early work was that he managed to underestimate the extent to which developmental and behavioural damage could be reversed.[12]

It is also important to recognise that the statistically significant "predictors" which pepper criminological research, rarely, if ever, approach the realms of certainty. In the National Survey of Health and Development, a combined measure was devised of factors that were significantly linked to later delinquency – including parent's social status, family size, child's birth order and suffering a broken home by age 5 – which still managed to miss 37 per cent of children who acquired a later criminal record. It also mis-identified 44 per cent of non-delinquents as potential offenders[13] (**Table 1**). Likewise, although 71 per cent of the boys in the Cambridge Study whose upbringing combined three of the most potent risk factors – low income, a parent with a criminal record and poor parenting skills – *did* later acquire a criminal record, that triad of predictors only identified a minority of all the boys who were eventually convicted or cautioned.[14] In New Zealand, although a computer analysis taking the ratings of children's pre-school behaviour correctly classified 66 per cent of those who were delinquent at age 15, it also picked out a much larger number of children who did not later find themselves in trouble with the police.[15]

17

Table 1 **Discrimination of delinquents and non-delinquents** (actual numbers)*		
	Predicted as delinquent	**Predicted as non-delinquent**
Actually delinquent	136	50
Not in fact delinquent	711	915
* Using data on birth order, family size and growth, parental divorce, separation or death by this child's fifth birthday, prolonged or frequent hospital admission by this age, social group		
Source Wadsworth, M. (1979)		

None of this invalidates an understanding that family and social factors are of special importance in the context of delinquency. This is even more the case with recidivists whose persistent offending accounts for such a high proportion of known crime.[16] The Cambridge Study found that children rated especially troublesome or unsuccessful at school or who came from families where income was exceptionally low, or homes where parental behaviour was exceptionally poor, were later heavily over-represented among the most persistent offenders.[17]

But the number of "false positives" achieved by this and other analyses does demonstrate the dangers that would surround an over-zealous crime prevention programme that set about stigmatising individual children and their parents known to be statistically "at risk". It also suggests that the search for practical applications needs to distinguish carefully between factors that are only weakly correlated with delinquency, those whose effects are indirect and those whose strength approaches that of a causative link. That is what the remainder of this chapter seeks to do.

Social status and income

Children from low income, working-class families are more likely to become delinquent than those from comfortable, middle-class homes. That much emerges from official crime figures and from the longitudinal research described in the previous chapter.

Yet conventional measurements of socio-economic status, based on a classification of a parent's (usually father's) occupation, have yielded weaker, less consistent links with juvenile offending than more specific definitions of poverty.[18] Michael Wadsworth and colleagues on the National Survey of Health and Development devised a modified version of class called "social group"[19] which showed that convictions for serious offending, especially violence, were most common among sons of the least skilled and educated manual workers.[20] The South Londoners in the Cambridge Study were already working-class in the conventional sense, but researchers found that a straightforward measure of low income produced less equivocal results. At age 18, boys from "poor" families were twice as likely to have a criminal record as those whose family income was judged "adequate" or "comfortable".[21] Recidivists with two or more convictions stood out even more starkly: one in five came from a background of low income compared to one in eighteen among the rest.[22] Pursuing the lives of a more recent generation, the Child Health and Education Study (CHES) of over 13,000 British children born in 1970, has confirmed that anti-social and neurotic behaviour in pre-school children is consistently associated with social disadvantage.[23]

Some controversy has arisen over self-report surveys of juvenile offending where the relationship between social class and delinquency has appeared especially weak. In the United States, 30 years ago, Ivan Nye found that socio-economic status was linked to criminal records, but not to self-reported offending. There have been subsequent claims based on self-report data that the social class connection is a red herring[24] or "a myth".[25] Most recently, a self-report study of children in four Edinburgh secondary schools not only exposed disturbingly high levels of victimisation, but also led the authors to maintain that delinquency *"could not be regarded as the preserve of any particular group or section of young people."*[26]

A possibility exists that some children from poor neighbourhoods do find themselves labelled "bad kids" and attract more attention from police than equally guilty sons of the middle-classes. Police may also display disproportionate interest in children of parents with criminal records or who live on "problem" estates where low income families are concentrated. Yet the important connection which Wadsworth[27] found in Britain between low social status and the *seriousness* of juvenile offences is actually supported by self-report studies.[28] In the Edinburgh survey, for example, involvement in offences like car theft, burglary and injurious assault was more commonly reported by children attending schools in socially disadvantaged neighbourhoods than by those in middle-class areas.[29] Yet participation in less serious offences – especially "incivilities" like rowdiness in the streets – was claimed by over half the children in all of the four schools under scrutiny.[30] Hence, although the total volume of anti-social behaviour recorded in self-report studies may not reveal a significant social class bias, that does not appear to be true of crimes that most people would regard as serious.[31]

Family deprivation in the context of delinquency can be viewed as a cluster of adverse circumstances which include inadequate housing and a poor local environment as well as matters of hard cash.[32] The mechanism by which these external pressures on a family translate into aggression or dishonesty among children cannot be a direct one. There is, however, a *prima facie* case for regarding economic and environmental deprivation as powerful **stress factors** which conspire to make it more difficult to be an effective parent. Harriett Wilson, for example, not only found that the most socially handicapped mothers tended to exert the least supervision, but that those in the inner city found it harder to keep track of their children than did their equally impoverished counterparts in the suburbs.[33] The Cambridge Study, meanwhile, found only half the rate of delinquency among boys whose families moved out of London during the first 21 years compared with those who remained.[34]

The most recent evidence of the way that social stress influences children's behaviour through parenting comes from America's West Coast. The Oregon Social Learning Center (OSLC) has based its research programme – uniquely – on observing relationships between parents and children as they unfold in their own homes.[35] Fly-on-the-wall monitoring takes notice of positive interaction, praising and encouragement by parents and of negative exchanges, notably continual "nattering" – a word chosen to describe the increasingly coercive situation where a parent continually scolds a child, who either answers back or disobediently takes no notice. Assessments of parental supervision, discipline and the consistency with which it was applied are also made.

From a longitudinal research project[36] focused on 10-year old boys (using criminal records and self-report data) it emerged that the statistical connection between socio-economic status and the children's early delinquency was *entirely* mediated by family management practices. In other words, social pressures were affecting the way that parents behaved, and that in turn affected the behaviour of their children.[37]

Divorce

Both recorded crime and divorce in Britain increased rapidly during the 1960s and 1970s. The fact that the former continued rising in the 1980s while the latter reached a plateau is, however, immediate caution against assuming that the two are intimately connected.

The extent to which marital breakdown and delinquency are related is, in fact, a rich source of confusion. In the words of Michael Rutter and Henri Giller, it is *"remarkably difficult to determine"*.[38] An attempt to draw statistically valid conclusions from 50 American and European studies of the subject has demonstrated that the discernible effects of family break-up on delinquency have not altered greatly in over 60 years.[39] Since divorce has become much more common and rather less stigmatised, this lack of change is remarkable. The "meta-analysis" goes on to suggest that delinquent behaviour could be 10 to 15 per cent more prevalent in broken homes than those where children live with both natural parents. Correlations are stronger, however, in the case of truancy, running away from home, under-age smoking and drinking – so-called "status offences" – than for crime in any serious sense.

The authors also found no consistent evidence that children in families broken by divorce were more deviant than those who had suffered bereavement or that living in a step-family made matters significantly worse. These findings are, however, at odds with results from research recently published in Britain and the USA. Data from the longitudinal Oregon Youth Study, for example, suggests that teenage boys living in step-families are twice as likely to be arrested as children whose parents are together. Boys who had experienced divorce by the age of 10 were observed to exhibit more behavioural problems than children in intact families, but those living with a step-father were even more likely to be anti-social, to suffer from low self-esteem or depression; to experiment with drugs, to have delinquent friends and to perform poorly in school.[40]

This picture of deleterious effects accompanying a series of "transitions" in family status accords with studies using the National Child Development Study (NCDS) of 17,000 British children born in 1958. Criminal records have never been examined for this cohort, but Kathleen Kiernan found that the risks of other disadvantageous events occurring, such as teenage pregnancy or leaving home because of ill-feeling, were higher in lone-parent families caused by divorce than in intact families, and greater still in step-families.[41]

Kiernan's work also makes it clear that the ill effects which children derive from their parents separating and forming new relationships do not occur as some sudden or short-lived reaction to the

19

acts of divorce or remarriage themselves. They are felt and developed over a period of time. Taking the NCDS in Britain and the more recent U.S. National Survey of Children, she and American colleagues demonstrated that marital conflict can lead to behaviour and learning problems for children regardless of whether their parents eventually separate.[42]

The National Survey of Health and Development drew a distinction in terms of the effect on children between the suddenness of a parent's death, and divorce, which could be "seen to be coming". Experience of separation and divorce was found to be associated with more serious offending than bereavement.[43] Likewise, the Cambridge Study in Delinquent Development discovered that boys from homes broken by death were not particularly prone to delinquency, whereas those who had been through their parent's separation were at double the risk faced by boys from unbroken homes.[44] Yet it was the family discord surrounding separation, rather than divorce itself, that was largely thought to explain the links with delinquency.[45]

Michael Rutter has portrayed divorce for some families as a painful, but necessary step towards limiting the psychological and behavioural damage caused by discord. *"In the long term (meaning over several years) most families are better off with divorce than with unabating discord and quarrelling, but things frequently get worse before they get better."*[46]

American research also demonstrates that homes which are intact, but unhappy and neglectful, are more likely to produce delinquents than those which are "broken", but where the children are consistently nurtured and loved.[47] The "direct" influence on children's behaviour is, again, seen to be the quality of the relationship with, and between, their parents.

Lone parents

Most lone parents in Britain are living with their children in the aftermath of divorce, separation or death. But an increasingly large minority are single mothers who may never have lived with the father of their child. What the two groups have in common, apart from the absence of a resident father-figure, is their poverty.[48] At any one time there are seven out of ten lone parents, including nine out of ten single mothers, who are receiving Income Support.

The term lone parent can, therefore, be shorthand for a constellation of social problems like emotional stress, financial worries, inadequate housing and isolation.[49] Such adversity is likely to be compounded by the youthful inexperience of so many single (never married) mothers. The widely held assumption that two parents are automatically a better safeguard against delinquency is not, however, supported by the evidence. There is, for instance, a very obvious contrast to be drawn between children who grow up in a loving one parent family and children who grow up in two parent families and are neglected or abused. Family structure – in this instance being raised in a one parent family – may once again be of less direct significance than the quality of care and supervision that individual parents are able to provide.

To take one example, as many as half the women included in a study of parents who had lived in local authority care were single mothers. Their own unhappy experiences in early childhood had, seemingly, predisposed many to become inadequate parents themselves; yet as many as one in four were judged by the researchers to show *good* parenting skills.[50] It has also been convincingly demonstrated that children who suffer indifference or outright rejection by one parent can still be safeguarded against serious behavioural problems if their relationship with the other parent is good.[51] Positive experiences in school can also help, to some extent, to compensate.[52]

The meta-analysis of 50 criminological studies of the behaviour of children from broken homes, already referred to, suggested that the statistical links with delinquent behaviour were at their weakest in the case of more serious offences like theft or violent crime.[53] Joan McCord, in the United States, found that criminality was no more common among children raised by lone mothers who were affectionate than among those whose two parent homes were tranquil.[54] The 1985 Home Office self-report survey of offending among 14 and 15 year olds, meanwhile, found no evidence that one parent families were, in any general sense, "criminogenic"[55] Girls in one parent families were less closely monitored than those living with two parents, but the authors concluded that life in one parent families was often more difficult, but not necessarily less caring.

Even so, the tendency for researchers to consider lone parents as a homogenous group could disguise differences between the experience of children whose parents separate and those growing up with a single mother who has never married.[56] Single mothers are the fastest growing category of lone parent, representing 6 per cent of all families with dependent children in 1991[57]. Their youth,[58] inexperience and poverty even relative to other lone parents,[59] suggest they may experience particular difficulties and stress in raising children.

In the absence of adequate research, however, it would be unwise to jump to conclusions. The instance of children born to unmarried mothers in March 1958 who found themselves part of the National Child Development Study helps explain why. At age 7, boys classed "illegitimate" at birth displayed poorer emotional and social adjustment in school than other children within any given social class. Yet the behaviour problems were generally greater for boys whose parents were cohabiting or whose mothers had subsequently married than among boys who still lived in a one parent family.[60] By age 11, girls born "illegitimate" and still living in a lone parent family had no more behaviour problems at home or school than children in two parent families and boys actually had *fewer* conduct difficulties.[61] Further research is merited to determine whether the children of young, unmarried mothers are, in certain circumstances, at greater risk of delinquency than other children. But there is already a strong indication that the picture could be more complicated – and possibly less conclusive – than some social commentators would like to pretend.

Working mothers

The second half of the 20th century has been one of accelerated family change. Women who might once have deemed it their role to stay at home with children now work either part-time or full-time in very large numbers.[62] Thanks to their earnings, dual earner couples with children enjoy incomes that are on average nearly 50 per cent higher than families where the mother does not work.[63] In spite of this, the "new man" prepared to shoulder his equal share of child-care and other household responsibilities remains a rare species in Britain.[64] The primary carer in all but a very few two parent families, especially those with pre-school children, remains the mother.[65] Most lone parents are women, too, but their economic circumstances tend to be different in that only four out of ten have any sort of job and seven out of ten receive social security benefits.[66]

Concern in the crime prevention world has focused on "latch-key kids" – children who are left to their own devices after school until one or other parent returns from work. Children who may be left unsupervised all day by their working parents during the school holidays are also the subject of increasing disquiet.[67] Yet there is no general reason to associate criminal tendencies with having a mother who works.

Fathers

Since modern working patterns have highlighted the limited part that men play in child-raising, it is logical to question the sexual bias in many criminological surveys which concentrate on *mothers'* employment and *mothers'* supervision. As recently as the mid 1980s, David Riley and Margaret Shaw abandoned attempts to interview fathers about their supervisory role on grounds of difficulty and cost. Yet their interviews with teenagers and their mothers very strikingly revealed that delinquency in boys *and* girls was associated with a lack of close feelings or understanding between the young offenders and their fathers. Studies of adolescents placed on probation tell a complementary story of teenage delinquents who need a "firm but friendly" father-figure if further offending is to be avoided.[76]

Exceptions to a relative lack of interest in fathers have occurred in the United States. Sheldon and Eleanor Glueck, comparing the families of 500 delinquent boys with those of 500 non-delinquents, found that fewer than half the former had sympathetic, affectionate fathers compared with eight out of ten of the latter. This was a far more significant distinction than that obtained by comparing the boys' relationships with their mothers.[77] Lee Robins, studying the former patients of a child guidance clinic, concluded that "anti-social" fathers – including those who drank excessively, were chronically unemployed and who had lost contact with their families after separation – were a highly significant factor in the backgrounds of children who grew up into anti-social adults.[78] A father's psychiatric status was, she suggested, a more important factor in predicting anti-social behaviour than his socio-economic status.[79]

Given that most offenders are men, the very fact that surveys identify having a criminal parent as one of the strongest family correlates with delinquency suggests that the role of fathers needs more attention.[80] Since the 1970s, the contribution that fathers can make to their children's cognitive and social development has increasingly been acknowledged and explored.[81] Myths that men have no natural inclination towards parenting, or that infants have no real interest in their fathers have been dispelled.[82] To take just one example from recently published research, the interest of fathers in their children's education emerged as a critical factor in the backgrounds of young people who successfully "escaped" from a background of social disadvantage[83]. Derived from the National Child Development Study, the finding is of particular interest, given the links between school failure and criminality.

Whether criminological research would demonstrate that growing up with a workaholic or uncommitted father who was seldom at home was linked to later offending is a matter for speculation. The role of fathers, not least in relation to older children, deserves more balanced – not to say egalitarian – investigation.

Heredity

The statistically strong link that exists between parents who have, themselves, been convicted of crimes and delinquent children raises the contentious question of whether criminals could be born, as well as made. The very fact that women, even in self-report studies, appear less criminal than men, suggests the need to consider a possible contribution from nature as well as nurture. The evidence for genetic or biological factors is, however, fraught with methodological problems and, at present, inconclusive.

James Q. Wilson and Richard Herrnstein have demonstrated that the gender gap in crime is real enough, but they hesitate to ascribe a genetic label. Their best guess is that, like other sex roles which endure through generations – and possibly more so – the difference between men's and women's offending is *"rooted deep into the biological substratum"* where change beyond certain limits becomes difficult.

Generations of the same families, identical twins and adopted babies have all been studied in attempts to discover whether a genetic element to crime exists. In one Danish investigation, children who had been adopted as infants showed a higher later incidence of delinquent behaviour if one of their natural parents had been criminal than if one of their adoptive parents was an offender. But children with both a natural and an adoptive parent who had a criminal record were even more likely to have been in trouble with the law.[84] The methodology of such studies has been criticised,[85] leaving the authors of a recent review to warn against trying to draw any firm cause and effect inferences.[86]

Criminality that might superficially seem to be inherited may, in many cases, be little more than the consequences of transmitted deprivation in which poverty, ill-health and educational failure are recycled from generation to generation.[87] But even supposing that some case could be made for a genetic or biological pre-disposition in babies towards aggressive behaviour and crime, there is every reason to believe that upbringing would *still* be central in determining whether inherent tendencies were encouraged or suppressed. As the opening section of this chapter argued, no child is predestined to a life of crime. People – initially under the influence of their parents – can and do change.

In the Cambridge Study, children of mothers who had worked full-time actually provided a *lower* percentage of future delinquents – possibly because their families were likely to be smaller and, thanks to mother's earnings, less poor. Mothers of the 1946 cohort who worked when their children were of pre-school age were a statistically very small group who did tend to raise more delinquent sons; but the significance was weak and disappeared once measures of social deprivation were taken into account.[68] Michael Rutter and Nicola Madge, reviewing the available research in 1976, added the commonsensical point that although having a mother who works does not appear related to delinquency, much may depend on the standard of care and supervision that a child receives in her absence.[69] The contribution that quality childcare could make to preventing delinquency is considered in Chapter 3 and the role of schools in Chapter 4.

Primary school teachers questioned as part of the National Child Development Study failed to identify 7 year olds whose mothers had worked full-time during their pre-school years as noticeably more maladjusted than other children – although their reading and arithmetic skills tended to be less advanced.[70] A more complicated picture emerges, however, from the Child Health and Education Study (CHES) of children born in 1970. A mother's full-time employment *did* carry an increased risk of anti-social behaviour in 5-year old children.[71] Yet the children of mothers who had given up a job during the pre-school years were also more prone to be anti-social or neurotic. Indeed, working mothers from disadvantaged backgrounds were less likely to be depressed than those who had no work to take them out of the home.[72]

What implications these maternal stress factors have for later criminal behaviour might become clear if self-report delinquency data that was gathered from some of the same children at age 16 can be analysed.[73] Nothing at this stage shakes a continuing view that the influence of family structure – be it a dual earner household, working mother, lone parent or step family – is relatively weak.[74] Like the stronger correlations that exist between later delinquency and low income and deprivation, their influence appears to be transmitted to children *indirectly* through their relationship with one or both parents.[75]

Towards prevention

In the search for practical ways to prevent children from growing into criminals, there is little advantage to be gained from focusing policy on the *structure* of families. The statistical connections, as has been seen, are either insignificant or the result of an indirect influence over the way that children are socialised. Hence, even if it were considered politically desirable to make divorce more difficult or persuade more women that their place was in the home, there is no reason to suppose that it would make much impact on delinquency. Indeed, turning the clock back could prove counter-productive if it threatened to increase the number of depressed and frustrated mothers denied the financial and social benefits of work and attempting to raise children in unhappy and loveless homes.

Other aspects of family life and upbringing display greater promise in terms of prevention. Among the most potent factors which research has linked to children's aggression and later delinquency are:

- *Inadequate supervision and inconsistent discipline*
- *Parental indifference and neglect*
- *Conflict between parents*
- *Parents who are – or have been – criminal themselves*

Despite a relative paucity of evidence about female offending, many of the same underlying factors seem to influence girls as well as boys – although the levels and seriousness of criminal behaviour are different.[88]

As a working tool for analysing the evidence available on both sides of the Atlantic, American authors Rolf Loeber and Magda Stouthamer Loeber[89] constructed four interlocking models which exemplify the influence that malfunctioning families can exert on children. They were:

Neglect – parents spend too little time with their children and are often unaware of any mischief-making. They fail to deal effectively with conduct problems like excessive arguing, bullying and minor thefts. Later they only hear of more serious behaviour from neighbours or the police. Even then, they may neglect to monitor their children's whereabouts and choice of friends. The children by then may be so used to "doing their own thing" that imposing discipline becomes exceptionally difficult.

Conflict – chronic disobedience from a child is matched by its parents' inability to exert control in a consistent, non-aggressive way. Frequent verbal threats and occasional unpredictable slaps fail to improve the child's behaviour or temper and may only serve to make it worse. The child becomes more aggressive with its brothers and sisters and – in extreme cases – may replace its parents as the dominant force in the family.

Deviant behaviour and attitudes – law-breaking by parents, or attitudes which reveal contempt for the law, encourage their children to act similarly. Parents fail to label serious misbehaviour as "wrong" and encourage children to settle their playground disputes by fighting. They fail to question their children's importation of property into the home which plainly does not belong to them. When police or neigh-

bours report misbehaviour, their reaction is to protect their children from the consequences.

Disruption – the life of the family is disrupted by chronic conflict between the parents or actual separation. The parents become preoccupied, irritable and prone to aggressive outbursts, leading their children to respond in kind. Parents under this kind of stress are less likely to teach positive social skills to their children or to deal with their problems effectively. Once the crisis is reduced or resolved, the children's conduct may improve to pre-stress levels.

As might, by now, be expected, Loeber and Stouthamer Loeber's meta-analysis of half a century of survey results found that all four models were positively related to conduct problems and delinquency. But the first three examples, all characterised by parents' inability to socialise their children, were backed by statistically stronger evidence than the fourth model, where the "disruption" to parenting was less likely to endure. The authors concluded that the time was overdue for parents to take up the challenges posed by juvenile conduct problems and delinquency. In an American context, they suggested a range of educational and therapeutic services which could be offered to parents on a voluntary basis.[90]

In Britain too, there have been calls to realise the potential for crime prevention through help directed at parents and families. David Farrington and Donald West in one of the most recent reports from the Cambridge Study in Delinquent Development call for a series of practical experiments:

"It is clear from our research that problem children tend to grow into problem adults, and that problem adults tend to reproduce problem children. Sooner or later, serious efforts, firmly grounded on empirical research results, must be made to break this cycle."[91]

The Cambridge criminologists call for action to tackle **poor child-rearing behaviour by parents.** In addition, they call for policy to address the relationship that they discovered between **poverty,** and between **educational under-achievement** and criminality to be acknowledged and addressed.

The next three chapters follow their lead. Chapter 3 looks at ways in which promising crime prevention initiatives could be targeted at families themselves. Chapters 4 and 5 go on to describe how schools and communities might join forces with the family in action to tackle delinquency and crime.

23

1 Nye, F.I. (1958)

2 Farrington, D.P.& West, D.J. (1990)

3 Kolvin, I.et al (1990)

4 White, J.L. et al (1990)

5 See, for example, McCord, J., McCord, W. & Zola, I.K. (1959) and Quinton, D. & Rutter, M. (1985a)

6 See, for example, Rutter, M. (1971); Hetherington, E.M.; Cox, M. & Cox, R. (1978); Emery, R.E. (1982) and Patterson, G.R. (1982)

7 See, for example, Olweus, D. (1979); Rutter, M. & Garmezy, N.(1983) and Olweus, D. (1984)

8 Or other primary care-giver

9 See Erickson, M.F et al (1985); Renken, B. et al (1989) and Egeland, B. & Kreutzer, T. (1991)

10 Bowlby, J.H. (1951)

11 Sroufe, L.A. (1979)

12 Rutter, M. (1981)

13 Wadsworth, M. (1979)

14 West, D.J. & Farrington, D.P. (1973). See also Loeber, R., Dishion, T.J. & Patterson, G.R. (1984) for discussion of a multiple-gating approach to delinquency prediction and Loeber, R. & Dishion, T.J. (1983) for a review of delinquency "early predictors"

15 White, J.L. et al (1990)

16 Just 23 boys in the Cambridge Study accounted for half all criminal convictions by age 25. Farrington, D.P. & West, D.J. (1990)

17 Osborn, S.& West, D.J. (1978)

18 Rutter, M. & Giller, H. (1983)

19 Taking account of parents' educational background as well as social status

20 Wadsworth, M. (1979)

21 West, D.J. (1982)

22 West, D.J. & Farrington, D.P. (1973)

23 Osborn, A.F. et al (1984)

24 Hirschi, T. et al (1982)

25 Tittle, C.; Villemez, W. & Smith, D. (1978) quoted in Currie, E. (1985).

26 Anderson, S.et al(1992)

27 Wadsworth, M. (1979)

28 Elliott, D.S. & Huizinga, D. (1983)

29 This was especially true of crimes involving dishonesty; less so of illegal use of cannabis and other drugs.

30 Anderson, S. et al (1992). Note, however, that even in the most middle-class catchment area, three out of ten pupils claimed to have participated in shoplifting at sometime in the past nine months.

31 Currie, E. (1985)

32 West, D.J. (1982)

33 Wilson, H. (1980) and (1987)

34 West, D.J. (1982)

35 See Patterson, G.R. & Narrett, C.M. (1990) for description of the observation methods

36 The Oregon Youth Study

37 Larzelere, R.E. & Patterson, G.R. (1990). A description of the OSLC's therapeutic work, including pioneering initiatives in parent training appears in the next chapter.

38 Rutter, M. & Giller, H. (1983)

39 Wells, L.E. & Rankin, J.H. (1991)

40 Capaldi, D.M. & Patterson, G.R. (1991)

41 Kiernan, K. (1992a)

42 Cherlin, A.J. et al (1991)

43 Wadsworth, M. (1979)

44 West, D.J. & Farrington, D.P. (1973)

45 West, D.J. (1982)

46 Rutter, M. (1985)

47 See, for example, Nye, F.I. (1958); McCord, J.; McCord, W. & Zola, I.K. (1959); Hirschi, T. (1969); Gove, W.R. & Crutchfield, R.D. (1982); Cernkovitch, S.A. & Giordano, P.C. (1987); Van Voorhis, P. et al (1988) and Graham, J. (1989)

48 Bradshaw, J. & Millar, J. (1991). See also Burghes, L. (1993a) for review of financial circumstances of lone parents

49 Described by West, D.J. (1982) in his overview of the Cambridge Study in Delinquency Development

50 Quinton, D. & Rutter, M. (1985b)

51 Hetherington, E.M.; Cox, M. & Cox, R. (1978); Rutter, M. & Giller, H. (1983)

52 Rutter, M. (1979)

53 Wells, L.E. & Rankin, J.H. (1991)

54 McCord, J. (1982)

55 Riley, D. & Shaw, M. (1985) described in Chapter 1

56 Burghes, L. (1993a) highlights the different social and economic circumstances of one parent families headed by single mothers, divorced and separated mothers and lone fathers.

57 General Household Survey. Preliminary Results for 1991 (1992) OPCS Monitor. Also Haskey, J. (1993)

58 Median age 24. Burghes, L. (1993a)

59 ibid.

60 Crellin, E. ,Pringle, M.K. & West, P. (1971) cited in Burghes, L. (1983b)

61 Ferri, E. (1976) cited in Burghes, L. (1983b)

62 Labour Force Survey (quarterly)

63 Family Policy Studies Centre (1991); Family Expenditure Survey (annual)

64 Kiernan, K. (1992b); Kempeneers, M. & Lelievre, E. (1992)

65 Kiernan, K. & Wicks, M. (1990)

66 Bradshaw, J. & Millar, J. (1991); Burghes, L. (1993a)

67 See Zigler, E.& Hall, N.W. (1987) for discussion of "latchkey kids" in an American context

68 Wadsworth, M. (1979)

69 Rutter, M. & Madge, N. (1976)

70 Davie, R. et al (1972)

71 Especially if the woman was employed in manual work. See Osborn, A.F. et al (1984)

72 ibid.

73 The data-set presents methodological difficulties - not least that it was gathered during the 1986 teachers' strike when only a third of the cohort completed questionnaires

74 A similar conclusion was reached by the Netherlands criminologist Josine Junger-Tas in a 1992 paper. See bibliography

75 Or primary carer, such as foster parent

76 Davies, M. (1969); Sinclair, I. (1971)

77 Glueck, S.& Glueck, E. (1950)

78 Robins, L.N. (1966)

79 ibid

80 See, for example, Farrington, D.P. & West, D.J. (1990) and Rutter, M.& Giller, H. (1983)

81 See, for example, Weinraub, M. (1978)

82 Young, J.C. & Hamilton, M.E. (1978)

83 Pilling, D.(1990)

84 Mednick, S.A.et al (1984)

85 Were, for example, the babies from disadvantaged and criminal natural families more likely to be allocated to disadvantaged and criminal adoptive parents?

86 Walters, G.D. & White, T.W. (1989)

87 See Wedge, P. & Prosser, H. (1973) for an analysis of transmitted deprivation data from the National Child Development Study.

88 See Loeber, R.& Stouthamer Loeber, M. (1986). Also Campbell, A. (1981)

89 ibid.

90 ibid.

91 Farrington, D.P. & West, D.J. (1990)

CHAPTER 3

Family-based crime prevention

"Modern parenthood is too demanding and complex a task to be performed well merely because we have all once been children" Mia Kellmer Pringle[1]

An introductory example

The toy library held twice a week at The Neighbourhood Project in Burley Lodges, Leeds, may seem an improbable place to begin the search for delinquency prevention initiatives. The excitement of toddlers test-driving push-carts round the floor while a project worker chats to their mothers is a scene innocently devoid of criminal associations. Nor does West Leeds Family Service Unit, which runs the project from a house in an economically disadvantaged neighbourhood. list crime prevention among its objectives.

The project is, nevertheless, in the business of preventing family breakdown and helping parents to raise children. In so far as its particular aim is to reduce the likelihood that children will fall victim to abuse and be taken into care, it is very directly concerned with preventing crime within families. Yet the reason that the project appears here, as an introductory example, is because of the way its work addresses factors which the previous chapters have connected with the risks of later criminality in children.

Activities at the centre include "drop-in" sessions for mothers, money advice clinics, a creche for shoppers, after-school activities for children and a holiday play-scheme. Specialist groups meet for women who are victims of domestic violence and young mothers who grew up in local authority care. Lone parents run a self-help befriending scheme and there is a parent-carer group where parents are advised on problems like toddler tantrums and bed-wetting.

Given the evidence that children's later offending behaviour is directly influenced by parenting and indirectly by marital conflict and poverty, it is not difficult to see how a family support programme that **was** designed to target criminality might contain some of the same ingredients. For example:

- **Respite** – the toy library and drop-in club help alleviate stress by getting parents of young children out of the home.

- **Support** – isolated parents can meet and share problems with others, helping them to gain confidence and self-esteem.

- **Parenting** – Small children are handled by the project staff in consistent, non-aggressive ways and parents are encouraged to become involved in their play.

- **Socialisation** – children are introduced to sharing their play with others.

- **Intellectual development** – children's learning is assisted by creative play and the encouragement that parents receive to share in play activities.

- **Diversion** – older children are kept off the street after school with interesting, supervised activities.

- **Protection** – at risk groups, like teenage mothers, receive special help with parenting problems.

- **Poverty** – money advice helps parents maximise their limited incomes.

The Neighbourhood Project introduces another thread that will run through this chapter: the concept of programmes which avoid stigmatising parents or their children. Some families are referred to the West Leeds FSU because their children are believed to be at risk of abuse. But far from being typecast in its catchment area as a place for "failed" families, the project makes a positive impact by opening its doors to all local residents.

Theory into practice

The practice, as opposed to theory, of social crime prevention is unfamiliar territory in Britain. Where existing projects are providing relevant services they are usually doing it, like West Leeds FSU, for different reasons. This view is endorsed by work undertaken for the Home Office which suggests that most parent and family support schemes are not directly concerned with criminality.[2] A promising base for practical intervention nevertheless exists among programmes which, for example:

- *Promote maternal and infant health.*

- *Educate parents, improving their skills and self-esteem.*

- *Provide care and stimulation for children whose parents are at work.*

- *Help disadvantaged families to become self-sufficient.*

- *Improve children's educational attainment.*

If they are succeeding in those aims, it is reasonable to expect that they are also exerting a beneficial influence over children's behaviour.

27

Research indicates the characteristics of families where children may be at risk of later delinquency. They are those where **abuse or harsh or erratic discipline** are the norm and where children are **neglected or poorly supervised.** They include families **torn by marital conflict** and where **low income** and external pressures like **inadequate housing** and a **poor surrounding neighbourhood** make it more difficult to be a parent. They may also be homes where one or both **parents have been criminally active.** All that information may be remarkably useless, however, unless the families concerned are willing to seek or, at least, to accept remedial assistance. As Donald West observed after studying the families of young offenders in South London: *"The least attractive and least deserving are those who need help most".*[3]

This difficulty might, theoretically, be overcome if preventive services were to be made available to every family. Such widespread provision might seem a little far-fetched, but it is precisely what happens with many preventive health programmes – for instance, ante-natal care and immunisation. Consider, too, that there are disadvantaged families who live in neighbourhoods that cannot be deemed poor and there are law-abiding, middle-class parents who still manage to raise children who commit crime. Delinquency prevention programmes that reached them would have to be very widely available.

At the opposite extreme, the object of social crime prevention policy might be to concentrate support on relatively few families selected by using the known risk factors. Yet even the most rigorous statistical efforts to pinpoint individual cases for treatment within the general population are far from infallible.[4] They yield too many "false positives" to make moral or practical sense of singling out young children as potential offenders. It follows that if families are to be targeted, then the most politically and socially acceptable method is likely to be that of concentrating support services on neighbourhoods. The selection process would be based on the geographical incidence of social disadvantage and delinquency rather than locating individuals at risk.

One exception to this would be those families who, in a sense, are pre-selected, because they have already come to the notice of social services or the police. Those children and their parents can not only be considered legitimate targets for social crime prevention initiatives, but they may also require the most intensive therapy and support services of all.

Three tiers

This chapter, and the conclusions in chapter 7, will argue that delinquency prevention work with families can usefully be divided into three different, but overlapping, tiers.

1   **Universal support services** which could be made available to every family.

2   **Neighbourhood services** targeted on high crime and socially disadvantaged areas.

3   **Family preservation services** for individual families of children who risk abuse or whose behaviour is seriously disturbed.

The structure is an illustrative device and its boundaries, as will become obvious, are fluid. In the interests of narrative flow, for example, a section on family therapy has been included under the heading of "neighbourhood services". Yet some forms of family therapy are not only relevant in an intensive "family preservation" context, but they also apply the principles of social learning that are universally relevant to parents. Note, too, that the Home-Start network – categorised here as a "family preservation" scheme might as usefully be described as a "neighbourhood service".

Like the West Leeds Family Service Unit, these family programmes rarely include crime or delinquency prevention in their terms of reference. Some are national organisations and others are on quite a small, experimental scale. Few, in Britain at least, have been thoroughly evaluated. They are, therefore, chosen as illustrations that give promising instance to the kind of family support work that could be adapted in a crime prevention context.

28

A social work perspective

Those involved in social work may wish to compare the approach here with the tripartheid structure of prevention described, in a child care context, by Pauline Hardiker and her colleagues.[5] The first division she made was between a primary level – where the aim is to prevent families from becoming formal clients of the social services – and a secondary stage where the object is to return the family to non-client status as quickly as possible. Her third stage of prevention is concerned with families who are in imminent danger of having their children taken into care. This latter will appear very similar to the circumstances in which the "family preservation" services described below become appropriate. However, most of the services which this report groups under the "universal" and "neighbourhood" headings are those that social workers, adopting Hardiker's structure, would ascribe most readily to "primary prevention".[6]

Universal support services

Parent education

When a baby is expected a panoply of services becomes available to the mother-to-be. Doctors and midwives monitor her pregnancy and there are free books full of useful information from the Health Education Authority. This preventive medical support extends into the baby's early life at home. The important work of Health Visitors recognises that new parents need and normally welcome the reassurance, help and advice that others can provide. It may, therefore, seem strange that parents finding their way through subsequent stages of their child's development are so often left to fend for themselves.

The view that it is illogical and unreasonable to expect parents to cope instinctively with the modern day stresses of raising children was aptly expressed by the late Mia Kellmer Pringle.[7] Her work was followed in the 1980s by Gillian Pugh and Erica De'Ath who examined just what education and support services were available to parents. As they put it:

> "Parenthood today is a demanding and at times stressful, lonely and frustrating experience; and if society continues to put high expectations on parents, then it must also provide sufficient support to enable them to fulfil their obligations with knowledge, understanding and enjoyment."[8]

The words "crime" and "criminality" do not feature in their report, yet its concern with making parenthood an easier, more satisfying task is of direct relevance. The 1990s have done nothing to diminish their arguments in favour of a "life-cycle" approach to parent education. This extends from birth control advice and preparation for family life classes in schools to support services for the parents of turbulent teenagers. Pugh and De'Ath stressed the need to make programmes that are sensitive to cultural and ethnic needs. Their further emphasis on the need for men to make shared parenting a reality has a particular resonance in the context of preventing delinquency.

Regrettably, their criticism of the lack of a coherent national strategy on parent education remains as valid as it was a decade ago. Preparation for family life has not been included in the National Curriculum. Nor have financially embarrassed social services departments shown great inclination to divert increasingly scarce resources away from expensive crisis intervention with children "at risk", in favour of preventive work with families.

Parent Network – Parent Link

One step towards providing parent education has been the emergence, since 1986, of the national voluntary organisation called Parent Network. Described as existing *"for any adult keen to change or improve their relationship with others – young and old"* it aims to *"help improve the quality of family life and reduce the likelihood of family breakdown or divorce."* One of the organisers simply describes it as *"a toolkit for parents"*. The basic training programme, known as Parent Link, is offered to groups of up to a dozen and starts by trying to banish any feeling that they should strive to be "perfect parents". Learning to listen to children, acknowledging their feelings and negotiating problems with them, forms part of the 12-week curriculum, as does building parents' self-esteem and ensuring that their own needs are not submerged beneath infant demands.

Of interest in the context of delinquency is the emphasis placed on consistent but non-physical styles of discipline. Parents are urged to be specific when confronting children over "unacceptable" behaviour and to enlist their help in resolving it. As the course notes put it: *"Each time we challenge our children and ask for their help in meeting our needs we are encouraging them to learn social behaviour that will stand them in good stead as they grow up."*[9] The encouragement given to assertive "I-messages" – parents stating clearly what they do and do not like – connects Parent Network to the more established parent education movement in America, notably Parent Effectiveness Training (PET), and Systematic Training for Effective Parenthood (STEP) in Canada. Research claims made for the best American support programmes are that provided parents persist with the skills they have learned they can produce lower rates of child abuse and neglect, improved school attendance, better academic achievement and lower rates of delinquency.[10] Criticisms of the worst programmes have ranged from a lack of theoretical framework to a tendency to make parents feel dependent, self-conscious and guilty.[11] Parent Network has, however, adapted American experience to a British setting, by placing training in a group led by a purpose-trained rather than a professional "teacher" and allowing time for parents to share their current anxieties and experiences in applying particular techniques.

Anecdotal evidence, in the absence of evaluation, suggests participants may, at the very least, feel calmer, happier and more self-confident with their children. Parent Network's organisers admit that growth has not been as rapid as hoped and that a peculiarly British sense of privacy about the family and resistance to being open about feelings may be partly to blame. The social profile of parents who own solutions. A research project is underway, sponsored by the Department of Health, to investigate the needs of African, Caribbean and Asian families, and to organise parent support groups. The organisation is also pioneering a workplace family advice service, particularly aimed at young mothers and fathers whose employment means they may miss out on support services available in the community.[13]

Exploring Parenthood's helpline enables parents who feel under pressure to arrange for a free telephone session with a trained counsellor. Limited funds have restricted the scheme, but it answers between 80 and 90 calls a month. Feedback from parents is said to be positive, but no formal evaluation has yet taken place.

Mass media

Some proponents of parent education have expressed a view that its full potential can only be unlocked in Britain with mass media involvement. Television, radio and video courses in parenting might not only reach millions of homes, but would create a climate where the need to learn about parenting was more widely accepted.

Open University

Between 1976 and 1986, the Open University's Department of Community Education devised a series of health education courses which featured parenting. The materials included booklets and video cassettes as well as broadcast programmes. The most popular course concerned "The Pre-School Child" and reached an estimated 151,000 people, including low income and educationally disadvantaged groups.

The philosophy behind the OU courses has been described as follows:

- *Parents have the best knowledge of their own situations – what they want to happen and what they feel most happy with.*

- *Parents have a wealth of experience and ability to put into their families, but may need encouragement to recognise this.*

- *Most parents feel inadequate at times and need help to build confidence in their own ability.*

- *With support, parents can critically examine and learn from expert opinion and theory.*

- *Through a process of reflection and action, parents can be helped to build up their skills.*

- *Building skills and confidence in parents leads to them taking a more active role in the wider community.*

have taken part has been heavily weighted towards the middle classes (75% ABC1s). One in four participants has been a lone parent, but only 15% of those taking part have been men. Success is, however, claimed for groups geared to the needs of parents from Asian and Caribbean ethnic backgrounds.

Exploring Parenthood

This professional-based organisation combines a national telephone helpline, offering advice and counselling to parents, with group counselling programmes for those experiencing specific difficulties. Its declared aim is to make a psychological understanding of child and family development accessible to any parent who needs it.

At the time of writing, an experimental "Parents Against Crime" group was being formed in association with police, social services, church and community groups in Kensington, London. A six-week course is offered to parents of 10 to 14 year olds who have come to the attention of the police. The groups provide parents with information about the juvenile justice system and education in how to provide a more positive influence over their children's behaviour.

Other work includes groups for mothers whose toddlers show behaviour problems. Many of the strategies, like those of Parent Link, make use of assertiveness training, stress management, learning to talk to children and listening skills. The assumption is that with skilled support over a short period, families can be helped to find their

Follow-up studies of those who studied the "Pre-School Child" course found many learners said they had gained "a better understanding of children". Improved skills, changed attitudes and higher personal esteem were among the other improvements that were claimed.[14] An update of the courses is planned for 1994, the International Year of the Family.

Video

An American parent training course, using video scenes of children and their parents, has been promoted as a cost effective method of treating behaviourally disturbed children and helping their parents to an understanding of children's developmental needs.[15] One study compared the results of a training programme using one-to-one therapy with those of a video-based course given to a similar number of parents, working in groups. Both led to sustained improvements in parents and children's behaviour. But while the individual therapy used 251 hours of staff time, the video discussion groups needed only 48 hours.[16]

In Britain, Dr Stephen Scott, Clinical Lecturer in Child and Adolescent Psychiatry at the Institute of Psychiatry, is in the first stages of applying this approach to the parents of 3 to 8 year olds with severe behavioural problems, including those that have been excluded from primary school or "statemented" as being in need of special education. A trial of a 12 week course using videos dubbed by British actors is planned. If successful, Dr Scott has suggested that the video approach could be applied at relatively modest cost as part of a national parent training initiative or for initiatives targeted on disadvantaged neighbourhoods.[17]

Dr Scott also belongs to a team at the Maudsley Hospital's Department of Child and Adolescent Psychiatry in London which has introduced and modified an American parental skills training programme known as the "Parent-Child Game". This work – often with families that have been referred in circumstances of abuse or neglect – is described later in this chapter.

Childcare

Childcare has come to be seen as an essential component of support services for the family. Its importance is formally recognised in the 1989 Children Act which not only seeks to regulate standards, but also requires local authorities to carry out audits of the childcare facilities in their area.[18]

Calls for more investment in childcare have been justified on various social and economic grounds, most notably those of encouraging women's employment and equal opportunities. The role of childcare in a strategy for social crime prevention should not, however, be overlooked. There is little evidence that young children with working mothers are more likely to become delinquent. But, as noted in Chapter 2, it remains important that the alternative care they receive during working hours is of a high quality. Accessible childcare that can keep very young children intellectually stimulated and well supervised may also serve to counteract the worst effects of family poverty and disadvantage.[19]

Many mothers in Britain, especially lone parents, do not undertake paid work because of the lack of accessible and affordable childcare.[20] But there are also indications that arrangements used by those who do work are inadequate.[21] With regard to the shortage of after-school care for children over 5, the guidance and regulations accompanying the Children Act suggest that one in five primary school children return home to an empty house.[22] This is of particular concern, bearing in mind the significance of adult supervision in preventing juvenile crime.

Given the strong indirect relationship between low income and delinquency described in Chapter 2, the primary prevention benefit from better childcare facilities is likely to be achieved through its effect on family poverty. It has been estimated that 1.25 million children whose families live on less than half of the national average income could be taken out of poverty if affordable childcare enabled their mothers to work.[23] In Australia, a cost-benefit analysis commissioned by the government demonstrated the effectiveness of publicly provided childcare in reducing inequalities in family incomes and giving one parent families long-term protection against poverty.[24] Comparable findings in Sweden in the 1960s[25] led the government to set targets for heavily subsidised local authority nursery provision.

A further contribution that quality childcare can make to delinquency prevention is through its ability to provide children with intellectual stimulation. The part that pre-school education might play in preventing criminality is addressed in the next chapter, but it is clear that day nurseries, workplace creches, child minders and nannies have educational responsibilities that overlap with those of nursery classes and playgroups. While the National Childminding Association has set up a number of courses, there are concerns that there is still not enough training or support for registered child minders in providing educationally enriching experiences for children in their care. Nannies remain a largely unregulated service.[26]

31

Concern has also been expressed over the lack of intellectual stimulation provided by local authority day nurseries – which generally cater for children of families under stress.[27] Not suprisingly, such nurseries care for more behaviourally disturbed children than most nursery schools and playgroups.[28] The Child Health and Education Study found that children who had attended day nurseries tended later to have poor reading and numerical skills.[29] This suggests that much might be gained both educationally and in terms of behavioural development by improving the educational component of nurseries. Principles of parental involvement – described in greater detail in the next chapter – could also be applied.

While the need to co-ordinate the work of day nurseries and pre-school education services is emphasised in guidance acompanying the Children Act 1989, a national strategy for childcare has yet to emerge. There are, nevertheless, a variety of encouraging initiatives at local level. A number of authorities, including Salford, Manchester and Islington, have provided nursery centres where care and education functions are brought together. Strathclyde offers comparable "Community Nurseries" with an emphasis on involving parents in the management of the centres.[30] Some councils, notably Hackney, Camden, Southwark, Leeds and Humberside, have established units or have arranged for their education departments to co-ordinate the development of education and social service policy for children under 8.[31]

A number of neighbourhood centres in Manchester, meanwhile, offer free pre-school care for children aged over 6 months, mother and toddler groups and after-school care for primary school children. North Tyneside council, as part of an economic development and anti-poverty strategy, has started a "childcare shop" where parents can obtain advice on the services available.[32]

Neighbourhood services

Family centres

The term "family centre" is applied, confusingly, to different types of social service provision at neighbourhood level. Those that are directly controlled by social services departments tend to be housed in re-designated children's homes or converted day nurseries and are a response to calls for devolved, community social work.[33] Family centres in the voluntary sector reflect a shift in the work of Barnardo's, the Children's Society, National Children's Home and other major charities

from providing residential care to preventive work aimed at keeping families together.

Bob Holman, who has chronicled these trends, poses the fundamental question of what it is that these family centres are seeking to prevent.[34] The items on his list with particular relevance to delinquency prevention are:

- *Keeping children out of care*
- *Preventing children from having to remain in care for long periods*
- *Preventing abuse or neglect*
- *Preventing the effects of poor parenting*
- *Protecting children against the disadvantages of poverty and deprivation*
- *Keeping children out of custody*

A survey[35] in 1989 found 352 family centres in England and Wales of which 57% were in the statutory sector. In analysing their ability to fulfil their objectives, Holman characterises them under three broad headings:[36]

- *Client-focused:* commonly found in the public sector, they are dominated by professionals. Their services, such as nursery care, mother and toddler sessions, intermediate treatment or family therapy, are offered only to clients – most of whom are drawn from the "at risk" child abuse register.

- *Neighbourhood:* based in areas of high social need, they may make a range of activities like playgroups, youth clubs or advice available to local people generally. Volunteer helpers often play an important role.

- *Community Development:* the rarest of the three, trying to get local people to develop and run their own facilities and activities.

Holman argues that local authority resources are increasingly concentrated on the client-focused model where social workers supervise children causing immediate concern. Yet it is neighbourhood centres that come closest to fulfilling the prevention duties laid down by the 1989 Children Act.[37] Unlike client-focused centres, they do not risk being shunned as "the place battered children go" and are able to cast their preventive net beyond those families that are "known" to the social services.[38]

One recent study of family support services compared and contrasted the approaches in similar-sized towns in southern England. Jane Gibbons and her colleagues found that what the statutory social workers had in common was a near siege mentality:

"The social workers in the two research areas were probably not unusual in their views that, while strengthening the community's own resources was desirable, they themselves could not take much part without sacrificing their specialised work with individual families in serious difficulties."[39]

Exceptionally, the social services in one town had worked with voluntary organisations to create a network of open-access neighbourhood projects. Families referred to these centres appeared to make better progress over four months than similar clients in the other town.[40]

The neighbourhood centres succeeded in attracting a higher proportion of socially disadvantaged[41] users than of other families. That achievement needs, however, to be put into perspective, since only one in four of the most disadvantaged families surveyed and one in ten of all families with children in the neighbourhood were likely to visit their local family centre within a given year. Men were especially unlikely to use their services.

Adding delinquency prevention to the specified objectives of neighbourhood family centres would make sound sense. But more thought would need to be given to increasing their ability to attract target groups, including more fathers.

Family therapy

Family therapy has developed in Britain within the wider framework of social services, psychology and psychiatric services. The practitioners are often social workers in family centres, probation officers and other professionals who have added a family therapy training to their skills. Since the families referred are commonly those whose functioning as a unit has been adversely affected by conflict, divorce, re-marriage or incidents of sexual or physical assault, such therapy inevitably touches on factors that affect children's behaviour and later risks of delinquency.[42] Yet the primary focus has usually been on other objectives such as improving mental health, better school attendance or the prevention of domestic violence and child abuse. Some of the earliest and best researched therapy techniques, for example, concern the treatment of schizophrenia.

The premise of intervention is that families function, for better or worse, as a "system". Change effected in one member of a family can bring about changes in the others and vice versa. Moreover, anti-social behaviour, beliefs and attitudes may go unchallenged if they are shared and accepted as "normal" within a family.[43]

But there are variations in the theoretical approaches that therapists adopt.[44] Differences exist over whether behaviour or feelings should be the priority and whether to concentrate on immediate symptoms or to delve into the experience of previous generations. One overview of family therapy in Britain grouped the diversity of approaches under five broad headings.[45] These not only overlap, but can be subdivided as well. Gill Gorrell-Barnes in a guide written for social workers pragmatically recommends asking which approach will work best in a given context.[46] A further difficulty arises from the lack of comparative evaluation of results achieved by different approaches.[47]

Family therapy approaches with the most obvious relevance to preventing criminality are those concerned with the structure of relationships within the family and those that focus on behaviour and social learning. In the former, the therapist's role is to help families put a block on disruptive patterns and to suggest new ways in which the family members can relate to each other.[48] For example, a probation officer using family therapy has described the case of a 15-year old glue-sniffer, found guilty of criminal damage and assault on the police[49] whose previously ineffective parents were persuaded to co-operate in applying consistent discipline.[50] The author warns, however, that family therapy is by no means a universal remedy and that *"not all juvenile clients come from unhappy, disturbed homes where the family needs help with its problems"*.[51] Behavioural family therapy, meanwhile, tries to improve communication between the family members and build on their strengths by teaching problem-solving techniques. Parent training, as described in this chapter, owes much to this approach.

Among the examples below, the Marlborough Family Service Education Unit suggests that a non-dogmatic approach to family therapy is yielding dividends in the treatment of truancy. It is followed by a description of the Oregon Social Learning Center – one of the most innovative and best evaluated examples of behavioural family therapy in the United States. A more general application in the shape of the "Catch 'em being good" parent training programme developed at the University of Washington is also described.

In Britain, meanwhile, Dr Stephen Wolkind and colleagues at the Maudsley Hospital have applied American experience of parental skills training in an approach known as "The Parent/Child Game". Another training method of American origin is currently being evaluated in Oxford with parents of children suffering physical or emotional abuse.

33

Marlborough Family Service Education Unit

Part of the North West London Mental Health Unit NHS Trust, this project is jointly funded by Westminster City Council and run by teachers with a family therapy training. Its "structural" approach begins by looking for strategies which parents can adopt to ameliorate their child's behaviour, but then tries to move attention onto the wider family "system" over time.

Children, who are commonly under threat of exclusion from school, attend a remedial classroom at the centre part-time for up to four mornings a week. But in addition to monitoring their educational needs, staff are concerned with their behaviour. Parents and others with whom the child has a close relationship may be invited to attend some of the classroom sessions. They then find themselves encouraged to take part in family discussions. As the therapists put it:

> "Many of the families seen at the unit would never agree to attend for family therapy, but will talk about the problems their children are having at school and will open up to discuss difficulties at home."[52]

Meetings with families are held at the child's school as well as the unit. The aim over three months is for the children to be reintegrated into their schools and to avoid permanent exclusion.

There is evidence of success, but it is largely anecdotal.[53] The teacher-therapists believe that perhaps a third of all children who are unable to cope with mainstream education at the time of referral make good progress, and that another third do well enough to avoid permanent exclusion.[54]

Oregon Social Learning Center

The work of Gerald Patterson and his colleagues in the field of parent education and family therapy over 25 years has been extensive and exceptionally well-evaluated. Their research has identified replicable ways of working with "uncontrollable" children in highly dysfunctional families and it has resulted in general, easy-to-read advice for parents on encouraging good behaviour and using non-physical discipline.[55] The OSLC, in Eugene, Oregon, has also devoted considerable attention to delinquency – both in terms of treating young offenders and the outcomes for younger children whose behaviour problems receive treatment.

A unique feature of the work, as noted in Chapter 2, has been the direct observation of the way that children and parents behave in their own homes. Hand-held computers are used to monitor the frequency of different interactions – for example, when a parent praises, scolds or humiliates their child or when the child takes no notice, answers back, shouts, hits or throws a tantrum. From such first-hand material, Patterson concluded that parents did not deliberately set out to raise little monsters, but that they often had no idea how to send their children the right signals of approval or disapproval.[56] Children who got their way through aggressive disobedience – even at the price of being slapped occasionally – became trapped in a downward cycle of coercion. Research found that simply teaching parents to encourage pro-social behaviour was not enough.[57] They needed to apply some consistent form of discipline that would punish bad behaviour and weaken aggression. Hence, although the OSLC's therapists are adamant that children must be talked to, negotiated with and praised, they also teach the use of non-physical sanctions. These include banishment to cool off in an uninteresting room – "time out" – or, for older children, imposition of a boring household chore. The use of a "points chart" is also encouraged. Marks are awarded to children if routine expectations are met (like getting down to breakfast on time) and deducted for misbehaviour. Reaching a minimum target each day results in a reward, like an extra bedtime story or, in older children, extra pocket money.[58]

Using a score based on the observed incidence of negative exchanges between parents and children, the OSLC has monitored the progress of families under treatment. One clinical study of families of "severely out of control" children, aged 3 to 12, found two thirds had their behaviour brought within a normal range for children of their age, compared to only a third in a comparison group receiving other treatments. The gains persisted for at least a year.[59] Less encouragingly, a small sub-sample of children known to steal showed improvements for up to a year, but it was found they were as likely to be in trouble with the police by age 14 as other young "stealers". Reviewers have also noted with disappointment a drop out rate during treatment of 25 per cent among OSLC families featured in the early research.[60] This is nowadays put at between 15 per cent and 20 per cent,[61] but the need for a strategy to maintain parental motivation and skills would need consideration before launching any equivalent programme in Britain.

The work undertaken in Oregon has provided support for the view that parent training is likely to prove most effective with children under 10. Patterson reports a 75 per cent success rate with children under 9, but only 25 per cent with adolescents.[62] This is believed to accurately reflect the waning of parental influence over pre-adolescents and the increasing power of the peer group.[63]

"Catch 'em Being Good"

This parent training programme was targeted geographically on neighbourhoods of Seattle expected to have high proportions of children whose aggressive behaviour put them at risk of later delinquency.[64] Over 500 children aged 7 in elementary schools were assigned, in 1981, to experimental and control groups. The parents of those in the experimental group participated in a seven-week programme that taught skills in monitoring children's behaviour and the use of appropriate rewards and punishments. Parents were encouraged to make their children feel more involved in the family and to increase the amount of shared family time and activities. Teachers of the experimental group children were, meanwhile, trained in techniques designed to increase the level of *"social bonding"* between pupils and their schools.

In the event, fewer than half the experimental group parents attended more than one training session (including only one in five fathers). An average of 5.4 sessions was, however, achieved for each of the families that did attend more than once. After two years, boys in the experimental group were rated significantly less aggressive and the girls less self-destructive than those in the control group. However, the significant differences applied to white, but not black children. Hence, while the authors derive "limited support" for their hypothesis that improved teaching methods combined with parent training can reduce anti-social behaviour, the study highlights potential pitfalls. These include the difficulty of attracting and maintaining interest in a parental skills programme and the need to ensure that any teaching materials are culturally appropriate.

Oxford Family Skills Development Project

A one year feasibility study is, at the time of publication, taking place into the application of an American family-training programme concerned with prevention of physical and emotional (but not sexual) child abuse.[73] The method works with groups of families who are invited to participate in up to 15 weekly sessions of 2.1/2 hours each. Parents work with "trainers" in a separate room from the children – who are divided into two age groups. But there is a a "nurturing time" in the middle of each session when the families get together for songs, games and a snack. The aim is to improve those aspects of parenting and family relationships that are most likely to reduce the risks of further abuse. These are said to include: empathy; the appropriate use of touch; consistent discipline; an understanding of child development and a sense of self-awareness.

In the United States, Stephen Bavolek reported that in a sample of 121 abusing parents and 150 abusing children, 80 per cent completed the course. A year later, 42 per cent of families who had been formally involved with social services at the time

---

The Parent-Child Game

A team headed by Dr Stephen Wolkind at the Maudsley Hospital's Family Assessment Unit has adapted and refined an American model of clinical work with the parents of abnormally aggressive and disruptive children. Many of the principles are derived from Gerald Patterson's work in Oregon and his theory of "coercive" families.[65] The practice, however, is based on a parental skills training programme known as "The Parent-Child Game" devised in the 1970s by Rex Forehand and Robert McMahon.[66]

Once or twice-weekly sessions take place in a video suite equipped with toys suitable for imaginative play. The therapists not only observe the parent and child through a one-way mirror, but can also speak to the parent through a microphone linked to an ear "bug" (like that used by television presenters). The parent is invited to play with the child and, then, prompted on ways to encourage sociable behaviour, while dealing effectively with disobedience and tantrums. The parents are encouraged to use warmth and approval to reinforce good behaviour, and are themselves praised by the therapists when their actions elicit a positive response from the child. Techniques are learned for ignoring inappropriate behaviour and for the use of "time out" in extreme circumstances.[67] In the second phase of training, greater emphasis is given to discipline and to the use of clear commands and warnings. Instead of vague, over elaborate instructions, parents are advised to issue commands that are clear, specific and direct. Children can then be praised for their compliance.[68]

The Maudsley team stress that these "prompted training" sessions are an innovative element within more conventional therapeutic procedures for assessing families, setting behavioural objectives and suggesting "homework". The families are almost entirely referred by social services and include cases of child abuse and neglect.[69]

A pilot study of cases treated at the Maudsley suggested that behaviour improvements were being maintained up to two years after treatment and that families showed a high level of "consumer satisfaction".[70] Members of the team believe that although the therapy is staff intensive, it is effective in "high risk" cases where children's anti-social behaviour has reached an extreme.[71] One consequence of the Parent-Child Game being featured in BBC television's QED series in May 1993 has been the publication of a short but helpful booklet of advice for parents whose children are proving hard to handle.[72]

of treatment had been discharged, while only 7 per cent had been accused of further child abuse.[74] Interviews with the co-ordinators of the Oxford project, one of whom has worked with Bavolek in the USA, suggest that the early results, in terms of retaining families and outcomes, show promise.

Family preservation

When children grow up in abusive and severely dysfunctional families they are placed in double jeopardy. Not only do they suffer a lack of parental affection or control, but the neglect they experience makes them potential candidates for care proceedings. There are occasions when the immediate protection of a child from harm demands they be taken away from their natural family. But the frequency of delinquent behaviour and social failure among children placed in care – especially those who experience a succession of different placements – is so daunting as to suggest that alternatives deserve consideration whenever possible. The Home Office's National Prison Survey in 1991, for example, found that 26 per cent of those in custody had some previous experience of care before they were 16, rising to 38 per cent of the 17 to 20 year olds being held.[75]

The extent to which different types of care placement – and the length of time spent in care – influence offending behaviour is a difficult area that further research would help to unravel.[76] Such uncertainties do not, however, detract from the case for family preservation. Projects which can keep children safe without removing them from their own homes are likely to prevent delinquency and should also prove cost-effective.

In a British survey of the backgrounds of 2,500 children entering local authority care, Andrew Bebbington and John Miles found that over half came from poor neighbourhoods, three out of four were from one parent families and that a similar proportion had parents who depended on Income Support. The authors believed that these families were not merely poor, but also lacked the support of friends who could help them cope with the tensions of raising a family.[77]

One of the functions of family centres is to fill the void for inexperienced parents by acting as "resourceful friends".[78] For isolated, potentially abusive families under stress, however, the best chance of returning from the brink may be programmes that reach out into their own homes. In Britain, there are volunteer organisations which do just that, befriending families and providing practical assistance. There are also instances of help being provided through professional "family aides". From the United States there comes the innovative example of "family preservation services" – programmes which demonstrate that intensive services in the home really can make many care proceedings unnecessary. The sections that follow describe some examples.

Home-Start

Home-Start uses trained volunteers to offer friendship and practical support to families of pre-school children. The aim is to prevent family break-up by providing *"a breathing space for parents and elbowroom for many professional workers who refer families to the scheme."*[79] Health visitors, social workers and other voluntary organisations like Relate, Stepfamily or Gingerbread account for most referrals, although many families refer themselves.

Volunteers must have parenting experience themselves and their help extends from an extra pair of hands around the home to emotional support for parents who may need "mothering" themselves. Visits are usually once or twice a week, but at times of severe stress when children are thought to risk abuse, they can be daily. By building parents' confidence and skills and encouraging them to make other friends, they can gradually learn to fend for themselves. Volunteers, who are matched with no more than three families at a time, visit for as long as is judged necessary – often for a year or more.

From its origins 20 years ago in Leicester there are now over 130 autonomous, local schemes run by a paid organiser under a multi-disciplinary management committee and served by a central consultancy. Volunteers are, increasingly, parents who have themselves benefited from Home-Start and the organisers claim particular success in recruiting organisers and volunteers among ethnic minorities.

In the year ending March 1992, over 3,200 Home-Start volunteers provided support for more than 7,900 families, including 13,425 children under five. They included 1,092 children whose names appeared on Child Protection Registers.[80]

Whilst cautious about automatically ascribing the outcome to Home-Start, a four-year evaluation in Leicester found that 86% of children visited who were registered "at risk" stayed out of care during the research period. Referral agencies confirmed the overwhelming view of families that being visited by Home-Start had brought change for the better.[81] Jane Gibbons and Sally Thorpe also included Home-Start in their two-town study of family support initiatives, concluding that it complemented the work of social services with vulnerable families.[82] Volunteers were found to be well-matched with the families they visited and able to work with a wide range of different needs.

Home-Start is cited in the Guidance and Regulations accompanying the 1989 Children Act as a successful example of befriending services which *"offer parents under stress significant amounts of time from volunteers who are likely to be seen as friends with no power or tradition of interfering in family life and who may themselves have surmounted similar difficulties to those met by the family being visited."* Organisers agree that the use of non-professionals whose services cannot be forced on parents improves its acceptance by families. There is no pretence, however, that its volunteers are in any sense a substitute for professionals, with whom the tough decisions about neglectful families must remain.

Newpin

Newpin ("New Parent Infant Network") is a voluntary agency set up in 1981 in South London in response to high local levels of child abuse. Although originated through Home-Start, it has evolved its own, distinct way of working with mothers of children suffering actual abuse or neglect. Eight projects have been established in the London area, Gravesend and Bristol and demand has led to expectations that another 12 projects may be launched elsewhere in the next three years.

Help is offered to parents who may be either physically or emotionally abusing their children with the object of breaking *"the cyclical effect of destructive family behaviour"*. The training tries to improve parents' self-esteem. While this is taking place their children receive the help of a play therapist, benefitting from home visits and friendship.

Newpin takes referrals from a variety of agencies, including Health Visitors, GPs, schools and social services. Parents participate voluntarily and some difficulties have been experienced with social services referrals if there is a perceived obligation to attend.

The training is for two half-days a week over 38 weeks. Group therapy examining individual family relationships makes up a major part of the programme, but each "personal development" programme begins with a one-to-one discussion of the family history and problems. New recruits are befriended by mothers who have themselves completed the training, and who visit the home as well as providing support and advice at a drop-in centre.

Participants interviewed at the Newpin project in Peckham especially valued this aspect of the scheme. All the project co-ordinators appointed to date have been women who were originally Newpin referrals. The expansion envisaged will mean that some will have to be recruited from outside the network.[83]

Newpin is geared to helping mothers as "main carers", although a father's group is being planned. Because of the difficulties many of the women have experienced with violent men it is considered helpful to keep the sexes apart, so that anxieties about family relationships can be freely explored. For similar reasons, it is not considered appropriate to open the project to general use by parents in the neighbourhood.

The projects assist the parents of 0 to 5 year olds. While this allows preventive intervention to take place before children reach school, one of the Peckham co-ordinators perceived a demand for a similar service for parents of school-aged and adolescent children.

Research on one of the Newpin projects in London is said to show that none of the at-risk children whose parents have undertaken the training has, to date, been taken into care. Other benefits have included reduced mental health problems, lower levels of social work intervention and fewer visits to the family doctor by the mothers concerned.[84]

Family Aides

A number of local authorities and voluntary organisations have used professional family aides to deliver intensive home help to families whose children risk being taken into care. Lacking formal qualifications, their role is comparable to that of community carers and the period for which their services are made available is usually limited to a few months.

East Leeds Family Service Unit evaluated a scheme in which families were helped for between eight and 14 hours a week over three months, followed by a six week wind-down period. All the families had at least one child under five for whom care proceedings were being considered. They were selected for showing a low level of parenting skills, but being sufficiently motivated to want to keep their child at home if possible. The help given to them included housework, budgeting advice, emotional support and assistance with parenting, including play sessions and introducing structure into the children's lives.[85]

Among 27 "high risk" families who received help during a three year study period, the work with seven families was halted by children being taken into care.[86] Another four families had their children taken into care within six months of the aide being withdrawn. However, a year after receiving help there were still 13 families whose children had not been taken into care.

An unfortunate feature of the scheme was the high level of stress which the aides themselves experienced. It was, even so, concluded that their work could play a useful part in a strategy to limit admissions to care.

Family preservation services

The family preservation programmes developed in the United States – of which the Tacoma Homebuilders in Washington State and Families First in Michigan are leading examples – take the home delivery of prevention services to a pinnacle that has not yet been attempted in Britain. They involve the intensive use of social workers and other qualified professionals in the homes of families who are at imminent risk of having a child removed into care. A sense of "last chance" is considered important to the success of the work, since at least one adult member of the family must volunteer to receive it. It also requires an immediate response to referrals and the willingness of staff to roll up their sleeves and give practical help around the house. This "social service version of the medical intensive care unit"[87] is time-limited in Tacoma and Michigan to a maximum of six weeks. Staff work with no more than two families at a time, spending a minimum of eight hours a week, but in some cases more than 20 hours in the home. They are on call 24 hours a day, including weekends, and can call in specialist services as necessary. A limited amount of money is available to spend on essential items that the family may lack.

The therapeutic approach is designed to build on the values and strengths of families, especially the desire to solve their own problems and stay together. In the words of Susan Kelly, director of Families First:

> "What they don't need is someone walking in and judging them or labelling their behaviour and saying they're a hopeless family. What they need is someone to offer them support and help to turn the situation round if they co-operate."[88]

The records of Tacoma Homebuilders since the mid-1970s suggest that more than 70% of families succeed in staying intact for at least a year. This is a remarkable achievement given that independent assessments confirm the majority of families served are at genuine risk of losing children into care.[89]

Other American states have produced comparable statistics.[90] In Michigan, Families First has been adopted as a state-wide programme, redirecting 10% of its out-of-home care budget. More than 2,000 families a year have been helped since 1988, of whom 80% remained intact for more than a year after. Success rates have been maintained regardless of whether neglect, abuse or delinquency was the original cause of referral. The number of annual care placements has fallen by 22%.[91]

The cost-effectiveness of such work has been variously estimated between $2 saved on foster care and $13 saved on placements in secure or specialist treatment facilities for every $1 spent on family preservation.[92] The typical cost per family of Families First is put at under $5,000 compared to $14,000 to $86,000 per year for a substitute placement.[93]

It is conceivable that British social workers are already more successful in keeping children out of care than their American counterparts, but family preservation programmes deserve further investigation. Since they rely on intervention when care proceedings appear inevitable, they could be expected to dovetail with, rather than usurp the role of, Home-Start and other voluntary projects. Conversely, it would be misguided for local authorities to think of volunteer "befriending" organisations as a cheap alternative to intensive, family preservation services staffed by professionals.

The Michigan experience suggests that it requires strong political will to re-allocate limited social work resources to prevention, even though the end result may be highly cost-effective. The other main caveats could be cultural in terms of social worker reluctance to redefine their role and of family reluctance to have their home "invaded" by professionals. Keeping children together with their families also carries the risk of a public backlash in the event of an unforeseen tragedy. During four years in Michigan, one child allocated to a Families First programme has died as a result of abuse. That a media outcry was avoided is evidence of the widespread public acceptance that family preservation now receives.

In Support of Family Support ...

This chapter has demonstrated that positive family support work already exists in Britain of a type that could provide the basis for a properly-evaluated programme of social crime prevention. But it is recommended that consideration also be given to new ideas. These include the adaptation of innovative parent education and family preservation projects in the United States which tend to have been better researched in a crime-prevention context.

Legard Family Support Centre and Radford Shared Care Project

These two programmes run by the National Children's Home (NCH) provide innovative, but small-scale models of family preservation work in Britain. Both work with families whose children are at risk of being taken into care.[94] But whereas the Legard Family Support Centre in north London is a residential scheme – accommodating families in flats for an intensive, eight-week assessment with follow-up support – the Radford Shared Care Project in Nottingham supports families in their own homes.

As with parents offered the services of Families First in Michigan, the families at Legard know that the programme often represents a last chance for the family to remain together as a unit. All the children have suffered some form of physical, emotional or sexual abuse and the parents present a variety of problems including failure to manage finances, to carry out daily routines and to offer stimulation to their children – as well as difficulties with personal relationships. The mothers tend to suffer from low self-esteem which often appears to be a major cause of their inability to provide an acceptable standard of childcare.
Most of the parents themselves turn out to have had difficult childhoods and been abused as children.

The families are offered individual and group therapy, while a play therapist works with the children. Advice is also given with the practicalities of child-rearing and home life, including bedtimes, cooking, cleaning and budgeting. After returning to their homes, families continue to receive support from the project for up to six months.

The success rate in keeping children out of care is about 50 per cent. Parents who succeed in keeping their children tend to be those who have had some positive elements in their own upbringing. With a ratio of 12 staff to 7 families, running costs are inevitably high and local authorities pay £1,300 per week for each family referred. The project is, however, considered to be cost-effective when set against the long-term financial and emotional costs of placing a child in care.

The Radford Share Care Project, on the evidence available, provides a substantially cheaper model whose success rate in keeping 50 children of 28 families out of care over a two-year period was 100 per cent. The project began with babies born to mothers with children already in care, but was extended to other families with children at risk and to homes where a child was returning to its family after a period in care.

In addition to support from local authority social workers, each family was assisted by one of five "shared care workers" recruited through the local child minders register and an Asian women's project. After preparatory training, their role was to help improve parenting skills and their services were available to each family for up to 20 hours a week. Mothers on the project were also encouraged to take part in informal group work.[95]

An evaluation of the project by Nottingham University suggests that its strengths lay in its ability to offer appropriate support to families from different ethnic and cultural backgrounds. The workers were judged to have gained acceptance because they were seen as friends, not social workers, and because they worked from families' strengths, not weaknesses. As the researchers put it: *"It is not (that) the women who are seen as 'inadequate mothers'..don't want to be good parents – it is that their circumstances are such that they need help and support to do this. What is suprising is how little help is needed to tip the balance to enable the women to meet the social services standards of 'adequate mothering'."*[96]

The help that families received would, if consistently implemented, bear down on many of the direct and indirect factors associated with children becoming delinquent. Such work could still, however, be undermined if parents were denied support from the education system and from the communities in which they live. The way that schools and communities can help families in a programme of social crime prevention are considered in the next two chapters.

1   Pringle, M.K. (1975)

2   Knight, B. & Osborn, S. (1992)

3   West, D. (1982)

4   Loeber, R.; Dishion, T. J. & Patterson, G.R. (1984)

5   Hardiker et al (1991a) and (1991b)

6   ibid

7   Pringle, M.K. (1975)

8   Pugh, G. & De'Ath, E. (1984) An updated version is in preparation.

9   Parent-Link Part One. Course notes published by Parent Network

10 Halpern, R. & Weiss, H. (1988a)

11 Quoted in Pugh, D. & De'Ath, E. (1984)

12 Interview with author

13 Based in three locations of the IKEA furniture chain

14 Open University Dept.of Community Education (1992)

39

15 Webster-Stratton, C. (1989a)and Webster-Stratton, C. et al (1989b)

16 Webster-Stratton, C. (1984)

17 Interview with author

18 The Children Act 1989 (Section 19). The "Under 8s Guide" published by the London Borough of Hackney in October 1992 is a good example of how the Audit process can result in a helpful and accessible service guide for parents.

19 Also summarised by Junger-Tas, J. (1992)

20 Cohen, B (1990). See also Bradshaw, J.& Millar, J. (1991) and Burghes, L. (1993a) on lone parents

21 Cohen,B.(1990) and Cohen,B.& Fraser,N. (1991)

22 The Children Act 1989. Guidance and Regulations Vol.2 Family Support, Day Care and Educational Provision for Young Children (1991)

23 Cohen, B. & Fraser, N. (1991). See also Holtermann, S. (1992) for analysis of the costs and benefits of adequate education and day care services for Under 5s

24 Cass, B. (1990) Why Public Investment in Child Care Matters: economic and social issues. Lady Gowrie Child Centre

25 The Erlander Report

26 Unless dealing with children from three or more families

27 House of Commons Education, Science and Arts Committee (1989) Education Provision for Under 5s

28 McGuire, J. & Richman, N. (1986)

29 Osborn, A.F. & Millbank, J.E. (1987)

30 See New, L. & David, M. (1985) and Lee, P (1990) Who Knows Best? Scottish Child Aug/Sept issue

31 Pugh, G. (1992)

32 Cohen, B. & Fraser, N. (1991)

33 Social Services Inspectorate (1988)

34 Holman, B. (1988)

35 Warren, C. (1991)

36 Holman, B. (1988) and (1992)

37 See Chapter 5

38 Holman, B. (1988)

39 Gibbons, J. et al (1990)

40 The reasons why were not clear, however.

41 Measured with reference to family size, housing tenure, overcrowding, lack of amenities and receipt of welfare benefits

42 See Bennun, I. (1988)

43 ibid

44 Gorrell-Barnes, G. (1984)

45 'Psychoanalytic';'Systemic' (the Milan approach); 'Structural', 'Behavioural' and 'Brief'. See Street, E. & Dryden, W. (1988)

46 ibid

47 Falloon, I.R.H. (1988)

48 Reay, R. (1988)

49 The case dates from before the reorganisation of juvenile justice under the 1991 Criminal Justice Act

50 Ainley, M. (1984)

51 ibid.

52 Dawson, N. & McHugh, B. (1986)

53 ibid

54 Interview with the authors

55 For example, Patterson, G.R. (1976) and Patterson, G.R. & Forgatch, M. (1987)

56 Patterson, G.R. (1982a). See also Wilson, J.Q. (1983) for a lively account of this work.

57 Patterson, G.R. & Narrett, C.M. (1990)

58 Bank, L. et al (1987). See also Utting, D. "Baker's Rap" The Guardian (9th October 1991)

59 Patterson, G.R. et al (1982b)

60 Notably Graham, J. (1989) and (1990)

61 Author's interview with Gerald Patterson

62 ibid, reported in The Guardian, 9th October 1991

63 See Chapters 2 and 7

64 Hawkins, D. et al (1987)

65 Patterson, G.R. (1982)

66 See Forehand, R. & McMahon, R. (1981)

67 See Gent, M. (1992) for a more detailed description.

68 ibid

69 ibid. But note that the family featured in a BBC TV "QED" programme (5/5/93) about "The Parent-Child Game" did not fall into this category and was obtained through advertising, not referral.

70 Whild, P. (1991) The Parent-Child Game: a pilot study of treatment outcome and consumer satisfaction. Unpublished. Quoted in Gent, M. (1992)

71 Gent, M. (1992) and author's interview with Dr Stephen Scott.

72 Available from BBC Publications

73 The American programme is described in Bavolek, J.S. & Comstock, C.M. (1983) and Bavolek, J.S. (1984)

74 Bavolek, J.S. (1984)

75 Home Office (1991). A study of young male prisoners by Michael Little (1990) found a similarly disproportionate 28% had previously been subject to care orders

76 For example, work carried out at the University of Manchester on a sample of 100 boys born between 1944 and 1953 who entered care found that those admitted earliest and who stayed longest had better outcomes in terms of criminal behaviour. Minty, B. & Ashcroft, C. (1988). Pauline Hardiker observed that this "suggests that prevention is far more complex than strategies simply to keep children out of care might indicate." (Hardiker et al (1989).

77 Bebbington, A. & Miles, J. (1989)

78 Holman (1983) and (1988)

79 Home-Start introductory leaflet

80 Home-Start (UK) Consultancy (1992) *Statistics Report for 1991-2*

81 Van der Eyken, W. (1982) and (1990)

82 Gibbons, J. & Thorpe, S. (1989); Gibbons et al (1990)

83 Interview with author

84 Results of an unpublished evaluation quoted in Knight, K. & Osborn, S (1992) Results confirmed by Newpin, which has agreed to their being mentioned in this report.

85 Leeds Family Service Unit (1987)

86 In three cases the family aides were instrumental in spotting evidence of abuse

87 Schorr, L.B. (1988)

88 Kelly, S. (1992). See also Barthel, J. (1991)

89 Nelson, D.W. (1991)

90 ibid

91 Kelly, S. (1992)

92 Nelson, D.W. (1991)

93 Kelly, S. (1992); Michigan Dept. of Social Services (1992)

94 Or where children have been removed to foster carers, but attempts at rehabilitation are being made

95 At the time of writing, a group for fathers was also planned

96 Fleming, J. & Ward, D. (1992)

CHAPTER 4

Families and schools

Pre-school education

"Pre-school education is life enhancing for mainstream children and life changing for those who are disadvantaged." Jane Ilsley, Director, High/Scope UK

Four-year old Scott is talking on the play telephone to Sam, one of two teachers at the demonstration nursery class run by the High/Scope Educational Research Foundation at its headquarters in Ypsilanti, Michigan. When Scott arrived that morning, he told the dozen other children that he wanted to build an army fort using large, wooden building blocks. Now, having put his plan into action – and helped put the blocks away – he is encouraged to learn more from his experience by telling Sam how it went. *"It was pretty good,"* he explains. *"But we had to let the girls join in the army."*

The emphasis placed on getting children to plan their play and take responsibility for their activities is typical of High/Scope's approach to "child-initiated learning". So, too, is the pupil-teacher ratio (less than ten to one) and the insistence on a close working relationship between the teachers and parents. Research demonstrates that children who take part in pre-school programmes of this quality receive an educational advantage that makes them more receptive learners once they embark on compulsory schooling. But evaluation of the work done by High/Scope does much more than that. It suggests that the influence of pre-school education in disadvantaged children extends into adolescence and beyond, improving their chances of employment success and decreasing the risks of delinquency. Ypsilanti, Michigan is, therefore, an appropriate place to commence this chapter.

It is, nevertheless, ironic that recent British interest in the effects of pre-school education on family functioning, school performance and delinquency has been stimulated by American experience. Despite the prominence given by this chapter to US findings, America is not, in any general sense, a world leader in pre-school education. Resources there currently allow only a fifth of eligible children to participate in the Federal Government's 27-year old "Headstart" pre-school programme for low income families. Britain has 46% of all 3 to 5 year olds attending nursery schools and classes, and infant schools for at least part of the week.[1] Yet compared to other EEC countries, the UK's record is not impressive. France, Belgium and Italy have between 88% and 95% of 3-5 year olds in education.[2]

Interest in the very best American programmes is, however, justified by the attention they have paid to rigorous evaluation and monitoring. The availability of data that identify the elements of success or failure increase confidence that the benefits claimed for pre-school experience are real and of a kind that might be repeated elsewhere.

Project Headstart and after

Headstart was launched in the USA in 1965 as part of the Democrat administration's "War Against Poverty". Its aims were to improve the prospects of disadvantaged families by improving children's health and education and encouraging the active involvement of their parents. These goals were to be achieved through the provision of free pre-school education and health care for all children in families below a fixed level of income. The quality of individual projects varied widely and many researchers felt that the initial concept was naive and ill-conceived. No systematic attempt was made to analyse the needs of disadvantaged children and what was provided in the name of "free activity" was often poorly structured.[3]

Most early evaluations were carried out in terms of improvements in IQ – a limited measure which failed to identify widespread or long-lasting benefits. Headstart had more success in promoting health and nutrition. But, more significantly, it roused the conscience of the nation and created a wave of enthusiasm for early-years provision which has led to better constructed programmes. Headstart has won favour with successive political administrations.[4]

Headstart inspired a number of pre-school demonstration projects with a more clearly conceived strategy. Evaluations of these reveal that pre-school provision can produce important IQ gains.[5] The best-structured programmes have also overcome the tendency noted in research on Headstart for the cognitive gains to be eroded during school years. More recent research confirms that the best pre-school programmes affect the cognitive, psycho-social and health development of children, yielding a wide range of long-term benefits.[6]

The Perry Pre-School Programme

The Perry Pre-School Programme was the research project in Ypsilanti, Michigan, from which the High/Scope Educational Research Foundation grew. It remains one of the very few to have looked at the

43

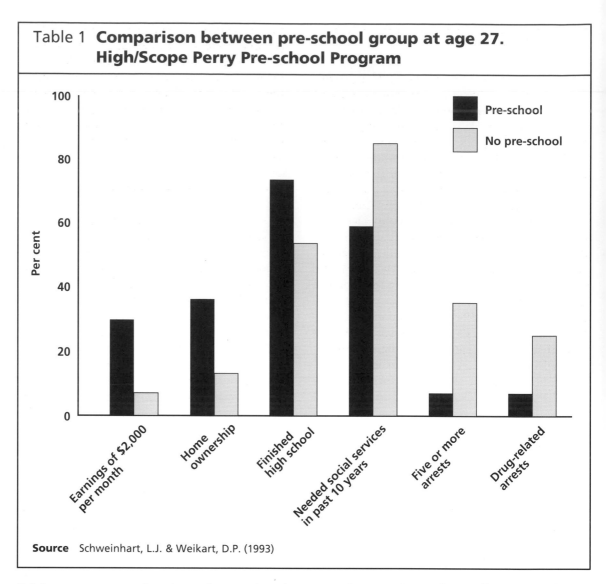

Table 1 Comparison between pre-school group at age 27. High/Scope Perry Pre-school Program

Per cent

- Pre-school
- No pre-school

Earnings of $2,000 per month | Home ownership | Finished high school | Needed social services in past 10 years | Five or more arrests | Drug-related arrests

Source   Schweinhart, L.J. & Weikart, D.P. (1993)

link between nursery education and prevention of later delinquency. Long-term studies of young adults from the town's black community who attended the programme when they were aged between 3 and 5 suggests convincingly that their pre-school experience helped them to achieve better literacy and, later, better jobs. They were less likely to drop out of school or be labelled as retarded and in need of special education. The girls were less likely to become pregnant as teenagers. Moreover, as was indicated in the introduction to this chapter, the Perry children had experienced significantly fewer arrests and were convicted of fewer offences. By the age of 27, only 7 per cent of the former pre-school pupils had been arrested five or more times, compared to 35 per cent of the control group.[7] (**Table 1**)

Although staff-intensive, a cost-benefit analysis of the Perry Pre-School Programme has revealed that such a programme could be an exceptionally sound investment for tax payers. For every $1 invested it was estimated to have saved the tax payer $7 in terms of reduced expenditure on special education, criminal justice system costs and lost tax revenue.[8] Research on other well-constructed early childhood programmes has demonstrated comparable short, mid and long-term results.[9]

Components of successful programmes

Coordinators of the Perry research at High/Scope stress that positive effects can only be found for high quality pre-school programmes which bring together certain essential components. These are:

- *A curriculum which allows children to choose their own educational activity within a structured learning environment.*

- *Systematic efforts to involve parents as partners in their childrens' education through home visits.*

- *Teachers trained in early childhood development*

- *Emphasis on meeting developmental needs*

- *Classes with 2 adults and fewer than 20 children*

- *A strong staff training and support programme*

- *Continuity with infant and primary school programmes*

The "child-initiated learning" aspect of the High/Scope curriculum, by which children are encouraged to plan their activities within a structured classroom session, is considered specially important for any delinquency prevention effects. One study compared three curriculum approaches: High/Scope's method, a more conventional nursery school, and a "direct instruction" class.[10] The High/Scope and nursery school approaches both emphasised activities where children pursued their own interests with staff support and guidance. The direct instruction approach, by contrast, taught academic skills and expected young children to respond to questions with the right answers. All three were found to have improved young children's intellectual performance considerably,[11] but by the age of 15, the two groups whose curricula had emphasised child-initiated activities reported only half as much delinquent activity as the direct instruction group.

Benefits

The Perry project was one of eleven pre-school programmes that participated in a "Consortium for Longitudinal Studies" in America involving 2,100 children. The main findings suggest that attendance at a well-run pre-school reduced the risk of school failure and increased the likelihood of completing secondary school and being employed.[12] The educational and social benefits for children have been shown to be greater in two year rather than one year programmes. It is also likely that even longer programmes would produce more stable short-term effects and larger long-term effects. The mechanisms responsible for increasing school competence have been identified as the child's positive attitude towards achievement and parents' increased aspiration for their offspring.[13]

Benefits for parents include less anxiety and depression; fewer medical complaints; more happiness; improved child-rearing practices and more appropriate use of health and social services. High quality programmes also lead to an increase in the use of other educational, health and social services. In programmes where there was strong community and parental involvement, it was found that other agencies and institutions became more responsive to the needs of the disadvantaged as well. Such "quality" programmes may be more expensive to start than provision that is less well staffed and equipped, but, given the potentially high return on investment, they make long-term economic sense.

It should, however, be borne in mind that the most positive effects of the American pre-school programmes have been achieved with children who are particularly disadvantaged and at risk of school failure. There was no welfare state on hand to support the poor, black families whose children benefited from the Perry project in Ypsilanti. The educational and preventive benefits for children who are not so socially deprived are bound to be less dramatic. A fair question, therefore, arises over whether the Perry Pre-school Programme results could be replicated in Britain.[14]

The answer must be a qualified "yes". First, the welfare state has not abolished poverty. There is no reason, therefore, to suppose that enriched pre-school programmes would not benefit the many thousands of children who are relatively and absolutely disadvantaged. Secondly, the Perry Pre-school Programme was planned to maximise the chances of success. It was, in a sense, overfunded and employed teachers with qualifications in both special and elementary education. This is not now thought necessary. The original Perry staff-child ratio of one to five was also exceptionally favourable. Later studies have found that positive outcomes can be achieved with ratios of one to ten.

Parental involvement

The Perry Pre-School Programme and subsequent High/Scope research stress the importance of involving parents. The family home is treated as the place where lessons learnt in pre-school are reinforced. Hence, teachers trained by the Foundation are encouraged to work closely with parents and other carers so that consistent messages can be given to children in the classroom and at home. There is evidence that teacher links with families are especially crucial when the children are small.[15] High/Scope in America has advised that family visits should be made once a week with emphasis on modelling classroom activities in the home. Home visits will not, however, be a component in four demonstration projects in Lewisham, Liverpool, Manchester and Newcastle-upon-Tyne for which the Home Office in Britain has funded High/Scope (UK), a London-based offshoot of the Foundation in Michigan.[16]

Involvement of parents as helpers in the classroom is also recommended, especially if training is provided. Some teachers feel that parental involvement is what makes the programme particularly successful. Statistically it is also one of the strongest predictors in American research of a child's future school success.[17] Engaging parents in their children's pre-school education is not, however, regarded as something that can be enforced, only encouraged.

45

Reviewing available research from a British perspective, Martin Woodhead has concluded that good pre-school education can *"engender, reinforce and sustain parental aspirations and interest in their children's education (which) appears to be a significant part of the ... process which converts short term cognitive and motivational change into long term educational and social competence".*[18] He found, however, that it was not entirely clear what form parental involvement needed to take: whether it should be encouraged by home visits and other direct intervention or by relying on the children's enthusiasm to trigger their parents' interest.

A major study of pre-school provision in Britain, analysing the experience of children in the Child Health and Education Study (CHES), found that fewer than half of the mothers had been involved in community hall playgroups attended by their children and only 13% of mothers whose children went to LEA Nursery schools or classes had helped in any way.[19] Children whose mothers helped in some way were better at reading and mathematics at ages 5 and 10 and had better communication skills than those whose mothers did not help.

The importance of links with parents was supported by Michael Rutter and Nicola Madge in their 1976 review of deprivation research. They argued that a main element of compensatory education for disadvantaged children must be measures to improve the parent-child relationship, family life and living conditions.

East Moulsecoomb Playlink

One of the main aims of a current British pre-school project – the East Moulsecoomb Playlink programme in Brighton – is to support parental interest through home visits. Each family receives a home visitor for one hour each week for a year. The child is then accepted into a playgroup for one term before going on to nursery school. The home visits encourage play activities involving the visitor, parent and child. The visitor also encourages families to participate in local community groups and two sessions are held each week providing a social opportunity for families to meet. The visitors focus on families' strengths rather than weaknesses and the emphasis is on shared experience rather than a "teaching" approach.

The project is open to all parents of pre-school children in the catchment area and currently caters for about 70 families. Research found that children taking part had greater self-confidence and improved social and educational skills by the time they arrived at nursery school.[20]

Pre-school and child protection

In America it has been argued that pre-school programmes should be used by the Family Courts as part of an alternative intervention to foster care for maltreated children who are not at risk of physical harm.[21] Clearly, a strong case can be made for combining the kinds of family interventions described in the previous chapter with quality pre-school and associated child health programmes. Such a strategy could be expected to reduce child neglect and ill-treatment and, thereby, address two of the important risk factors for later delinquency.

Playgroups

The High/Scope curriculum enjoys the advantage of having been thoroughly evaluated, but it is clearly not the only route to quality and effective prevention. There is already a tradition of good pre-school education in the UK – albeit not as widespread as in other European countries. It is probable that some facilities, including the best-run playgroups, achieve benefits similar to those of the successful demonstration programmes in the USA.[22] Playgroups are currently used by about half of all 3 and 4-year olds in the UK.[23] However, while they tend to improve children's social and cognitive skills, one comparative study of working class children found that those who had attended a nursery class concentrated better when alone, enjoyed richer play, were more independent and made better use of their teachers than those who attended a playgroup.[24] There was no significant difference in conceptual attainment between the two groups but the children who attended nursery school seemed socially more mature and eager to learn. This seems to support the findings of the High/Scope researchers who argue that children's attitudes on school entry are a crucial influence on later school performance.[25]

Analysis of the experience of children in the Child Health and Education Study cohort, however, found that there were few significant differences in terms of test scores between the various types of pre-school provision. The authors concluded that so long as a child had proper care, interesting activities and other children to play with, the actual type of pre-school provision mattered very little. The main contrast, they suggested, was between children with pre-school experience and those with none.[26]

It should be noted that their conclusions refer to test scores rather than behavioural factors. The few statistically significant differences they do cite are also worthy of mention; notably the low test scores of children who had attended LEA Nursery Classes in Infant Schools compared to those who attended LEA Nursery Schools. They also suggest that the unexpectedly few differences between playgroup and LEA Nursery Schools may be explained by differences in social background of the children and the levels of staffing and equipment available. Although LEA Nursery Schools cater for a higher proportion of disadvantaged pupils, they benefit from higher investment per child. The possibility therefore exists that nursery school serves to place less privileged children on a level playing field with the more middle class children attending playgroups by the time they reach primary school.[27] The plea, as ever, is for further research.

Reinforcing the benefits

Although pre-school education has enduring benefits that are directly or indirectly relevant to preventing delinquency, it would be wrong to think of it as providing lasting protection in the way that an innoculation does against disease. Rather, as Martin Woodhead argues, short-lived improvements in competence, coupled with increased motivation, parental aspirations and school expectations, trigger a *"mutually reinforcing positive cycle of achievement"*.[28] In many cases, however, the effects may only prove durable if support from the family and in school continues beyond the pre-school years.

Primary schools

"An effective school is one in which pupils progress further than might be expected from a consideration of intake" Peter Mortimore[29]

If early prevention is to have permanent effects, good experiences in a child's early years must be reinforced and built upon.[30] Good pre-school education involving families needs to be followed by good primary education involving families. The next two sections consider ways in which primary and secondary schools can complement parents' efforts to reduce the likelihood of their children offending. In particular, they focus on the mutually reinforcing links between families and school.

School effectiveness

During the past decade, there has been growing interest in the school as a means of reducing anti-social behaviour and delinquency. Until the late 1970s, it was widely believed that the differences between schools in pupil attainment and delinquency rates were largely due to the type of pupils

enrolled rather than what happened to them in the classroom. As recently as 1972, one influential researcher considered that "school" factors accounted for less than 6 per cent of the variation in attainment between students.[31]

This view has been questioned by recent research which found that some schools in high crime neighbourhoods had relatively low delinquency rates while some in low crime areas had disproportionately high levels. These differences could not be explained by disparities in the pupil intake.[32]

The idea that schools can exert an independent effect on pupil performance and delinquency has led to a reinterpretation of earlier studies which asserted the overriding importance of family factors. It seems likely that schools – as well as the influence of peers as children grow older – are more important than was once thought. It is not easy to prove a direct causal relationship between what goes on inside schools and delinquent behaviour outside. However, schools clearly exert a **direct** influence on truancy, disruptiveness and thereby on the success or failure of their pupils.[33] Those factors, in turn, are associated with delinquency.[34] Moreover, since school failure is linked with delinquency through its impact on self-esteem and the formation of anti-school peer groups, it is probable that schools exert an important **indirect** influence on anti-social or criminal behaviour of their pupils. No single feature of the functioning of schools explains this effect. Rather, it has been attributed to the general ethos and organisation of schools.

Translating research into actual school improvement programmes, however, has not been pursued with nearly the same vigour in Britain as in the USA where as many as half the 16,000 school districts have implemented a schools effectiveness programme.[35] Transforming ineffective schools into effective ones is not a straightforward matter and Peter Mortimore argues that a strategy for promoting change has to be adopted, which is likely to require outside help.[36]

Effectiveness in practice

The most important piece of research examining the effectiveness of primary schools in Britain found differences in the levels of attainment by primary school pupils that could not be explained by differences in the social background of their intake.[37] Factors which were found to characterise effective schools included:

- *The quality of leadership from the headteacher*

- *A consistent approach by teachers*

- *Intellectually challenging teaching*

- *Structured lessons*
- *A positive climate within the school*
- *Parental involvement.*

One purpose of current "effectiveness" initiatives in primary schools is to prevent school failure and – thereby – the risks of subsequent delinquency and drug abuse. Research suggests that approaches which target individual children have been less successful than those in which the whole school is taken as the context for prevention.[38]

One successful programme in the USA has been the **Yale (New Haven) School Development Programme (SDP).** Developed by Dr James Comer, it sought to ensure that school management was based on the best principles of child development. Particular emphasis was laid on parent participation. A planning and management team, directed by a head teacher and consisting of teachers, parents and a mental health professional, was established. The purpose was to consider problems and find opportunities for improving schools' environment, curricula and staffing. A group of child and family mental health specialists was also introduced into schools, providing a direct service to children, and assistance to parents and staff. Special effort was made to identify pupils at risk of poor performance in reading and mathematics so they could receive remedial help. A parent participation programme, meanwhile, brought parents into schools, assisting teachers on a half-time basis, and receiving a teacher's minimum wage. They took responsibility for organising events and encouraging involvement of other parents.

Comer describes his programme as a "process", rather than a package of instructional methods or techniques. It is credited with giving parents, teachers and children a greater sense of community. He likens the impact which schools have on child development to that of the family itself. *"They don't have their effect through the specific skills they transmit alone, but through their values, climate, quality of relationships."*[39]

The results have been remarkable. In 1969, the pupils in the first school to be targeted were 18-19 months behind the average for their age groups in reading and mathematics. There were also serious behaviour and attendance problems. High staff turnover reflected low morale. Yet since 1976 the school has been among the top five in the city in attendance and has not had a serious behaviour problem in a decade. By 1979, pupil reading and mathematics skills had risen to around the national average. Staff attendance was among the best in the city and turnover was among the lowest. Parent participation had been enthusiastic

with attendance at school events greatly improved.[40]

Involving parents

The relationship between parents and the primary school is considered by Dr Comer and his colleagues to be crucial. The message teachers seek to pass to parents is that education is a shared venture. Most educationalists would agree that a positive attitude by parents to their child's learning can improve their children's performance at school and that a good relationship between families and teachers makes it easier to resolve crises when they occur.

These beliefs are supported by research. The National Survey of Health and Development in Britain found that school achievement was greatly influenced by home background factors.[41] Parental interest in children's school work was found to be more important than any other factors such as the size of the family, the standard of their home or even the academic record of the particular school. All other things being equal, it was concluded that the major influences on a child's ability to take advantage of educational opportunity seemed to be his/her parents' attitude to education and interest in school work.[42]

In practical terms, parents can become involved by helping in the classroom, with extra-curricular events and with sports and after-school activities. Problems sometimes arise, however, from a lack of resources or training and from parent apathy and teacher resistance.[43]

Home visits and reading schemes

Home visits are carried out in a minority of primary schools, but more frequently in nurseries and schools with nursery classes.[44] Visits are valued by many parents and teachers and enable teachers to see families who cannot or do not visit the school. Others, however, feel that it places an unsustainable burden on teachers (who in any case receive no formal training in home-school liaison) and that there is a danger of undermining parental competence.

One type of family and school involvement that has proved effective has been the encouragement given to parents to help their children to read. Without requiring parents to visit schools regularly, this approach, using commercially produced materials, achieves a degree of collaboration with teachers. Evaluations have found that participating children become more advanced in their reading than those in control groups.[45] Despite its success, only a handful of local education authori-

Bullying in schools

Schools, as this chapter shows, can either consciously strive to inhibit delinquency among their pupils or, unwittingly, compound the delinquent tendencies of young people from vulnerable families. One important part of this process is likely to be their success, or otherwise, in the prevention of bullying.

Bullying – *"the repeated oppression of a less powerful person by a more powerful one"*[68] – takes many forms. In schools, it can range from deliberately cruel teasing and verbal abuse to levels of intimidation and physical violence that are plainly criminal. Studies in Britain, Scandinavia, the United States and Canada, all suggest that more boys are bullies than girls, but that girls and boys are equally likely to find themselves among the victims. Boys are usually bullied by other boys, but girls are just as likely to be bullied by boys as by other girls.[69]

The fact that child bullies have been shown to have aggressive personalities, to be below average in popularity and academic achievement and to have poor relations with their parents[70] connects them very clearly to the mainstream evidence linking family factors with delinquency. A longitudinal study in Norway, for example, found that 60 per cent of known school bullies had been convicted of criminal offences by the age of 24 and that bullies were four times more likely to have become recidivists than were non-bullies.[71] The former victims were, meanwhile, more likely to suffer from low self-esteem and depression in young adulthood.[72]

Results from the Cambridge Study in Delinquent Development suggest that men who are bullies as teenagers also tend to be bullies as adults. Childhood factors found to recur in the backgrounds of adult bullies included low attainment at primary school, having criminal parents, suffering physical neglect and having a father who did not share in their leisure activities.[73] The research also revealed continuity between the generations, in that men who had been bullies as teenagers were especially likely to have fathered a young bully by the time they were 32.[74]

There can be no doubt that schools and parents who work together to combat bullying render an important social service. The indications are that bullying is more frequent in primary than secondary schools, and that it occurs during break and other times when pupils are least likely to be supervised.[75] But unless schools take positive steps against bullying, much of what goes on may never be reported to either teachers or parents.[76]

David Farrington in a paper derived from recent work on bullying commissioned by the Home Office describes the "whole school" approach that was tested in Norway during in the early 1980s. The government-led campaign included the circulation of booklets and videos about bullying to schools and distribution of a four-page leaflet to parents. Although results of a three-year follow-up study were not wholly encouraging,[77] it emerged that schools which had been heavily involved in the campaign had a reduced incidence of bullying, which had increased elsewhere. Schools in Bergen, for example, issued questionnaires about the prevalence of bullying and encouraged teachers to improve playground supervision while making it clear that victims would be listened to. After 20 months, reports of victimisation had fallen by half.[78]

An anti-bullying programme funded by the Department for Education which is currently being tested in 23 Sheffield schools, builds on this approach. Pupils are being asked for their prevention ideas and "bully courts" are being included, where suspected bullies are brought before a panel of pupils and teachers.

Prof. Farrington, meanwhile, recommends that an anti-bullying programme in schools should include the following elements:

- *A confidential, self-report questionnaire for pupils followed by a school conference to discuss the results*

- *Providing teachers with booklets and videos about bullying*

- *Parent-teacher meetings to discuss the campaign and to seek ideas*

- *Better playground supervision*

- *Classroom discussions on bullying backed by a school policy making it clear that bullies will not be tolerated and that victims will be listened to by staff*

- *Teachers making special efforts to talk to bullies and their parents*

- *Appropriate sanctions against bullies, but also efforts to ensure that their good behaviour is praised in school and at home*

- *Action to improve victims' status and self-confidence.*[79]

Farrington further notes that in an experiment in Canada, the parents of disruptive six year old boys were offered parental skills training based on the work of the Oregon Social Learning Center (described in chapter 3). One result was significantly less bullying by the age of nine than was found in a control group of children with similar problems.[80]

ties have followed the example of councils like Haringey and Rochdale that have pioneered such schemes. The Sheffield Early Literacy Development Project, however, combines the distribution of learning material into the homes of under-fives with a programme of home visits and parents' meetings. An evaluation found it had improved children's experience of early writing and use of books.[46]

A National Foundation for Educational Research (NFER) study of parent involvement in primary schools identified further ways in which home-school links can be developed. Schools can, for example, support working parents by providing care and activities outside classroom hours. Some primary schools, meanwhile, rely on Parent Teacher Associations to involve parents. About 35% of primary schools have them but some headteachers are convinced that formal PTAs scare too many parents away.[47]

The NFER study found that, contrary to the belief of most headteachers, parental attitudes to education were not greatly influenced by attempts to involve them in the ordinary, day-to-day activities of their children's schools. Nor did increased involvement of that type lead to a change in parental attitude to school and thence to improved pupil attainment.[48] Since it is agreed, however, that delinquency prevention requires more parents to take an interest in their children's education, it would make sense to develop approaches which show the greatest potential for success. Efforts need to be concentrated on approaches which do not require unsustainable levels of teacher time and which have been shown to have the most educational benefit.

Secondary schools

Parents' ability to prevent delinquent behaviour at a time when their children are most susceptible will depend, in part, on the effectiveness of the schools they attend. A number of studies have tried to identify the essential differences between effective and less effective secondary schools.

The best known is that undertaken by Michael Rutter and colleagues in 1979 in 12 inner London secondary schools.[49] It found that behaviour, attendance and school success were significantly associated with the schools themselves and concluded that *some schools were better able than others to foster good behaviour and attainment*.[50] In trying to establish reasons, they ruled out physical or administrative aspects of the school such as type of building, or overcrowding. They found that it was "school processes" which accounted for the differences. These included the value accorded to children's non-academic skills; rewards and punishments; teaching methods; the stability of staffing and of childrens' friendship groups; participation in school activities and staff organisation. Their study demonstrates convincingly that there are features of school organisation which are strongly and consistently associated with attendance, school achievement, behaviour and, to a lesser extent, delinquency.

Another study considered whether "effective" schools worked equally well for children from ethnic minority groups. After controlling for background and previous attainment, it found that the differences in performance between schools were substantial. Moreover, these differences were greater than the relatively small differences in performance between pupils from different ethnic minority groups.[51]

Differences between schools are, however, seldom as great as the differences between the homes and family backgrounds of their pupils. It follows that effective schools are not going to compensate fully for the enormous differences between individual pupils in terms of ability and motivation. Yet the work done by the most effective secondary schools appears to "ratchet" up the level of educational achievement and make a significant difference to children's motivation, exam success and delinquency. If all schools could be improved to the level of the best urban comprehensives, it has been suggested this would be sufficient to transform the standards of secondary education in Britain.[52]

Summarising crime prevention research for the Helsinki Institute for Crime Prevention and Control, John Graham described ways that secondary schools might inhibit or promote delinquency. He suggested that:

> "... schools which are able to offer students a sense of achievement regardless of ability and are able to motivate and integrate them are likely to reduce the incidence of negative outcomes".[53]

He added that:

> "Schools which are likely to have high rates of delinquency among pupils are those which, inadvertently or otherwise, segregate pupils according to academic ability, concentrate on academic success at the expense of practical and social skills, categorise pupils as deviants, inadequates and failures and refer responsibility for the behaviour and welfare of their pupils to outside agencies and institutions. Schools which permanently exclude their most difficult pupils or ignore those who persistently fail to attend school, may themselves be contributing to the promotion of delinquency".[54]

In some cases, Graham suggests that schools need to review their own organisation and "ethos" with a view to changing the internal conditions which give rise to truancy and disruptive behaviour.[55] There are, however, limits to what individual schools can do, given their intake. Michael Rutter found that delinquency rates and truancy were *lower* in schools which had a relatively high concentration of pupils in the upper ability bands at intake and *higher* in those with a low proportion of high ability pupils although there were no significant differences in behaviour in school. It seems that schools with a high proportion of less able pupils can influence pupil behaviour in school by good management more than they can attendance and delinquency outside of school.[56]

Not all the research studies have been able to say precisely what it was about some schools that made them more effective than others. Some, however, have identified factors and suggested the route schools should take in order to maximise levels of achievement and minimise levels of delinquency. Some schools throughout the UK are already applying the principles of "effectiveness" with success.

Parent-school links

Persistent non-attendance at school is associated with juvenile and later adult offending.[57] It is also a problem that is apt to bring parents and school authorities into conflict.

Parents have diminishing influence over secondary school age children because of their increasing independence and growing tendency to accept the behavioural values of their chosen peer group. It is also more difficult at this late stage to foster a good relationship between home and school. The contact at this level has much to do with advice, guidance and dealing with absence. Although it is a different, more distant sort of involvement to that which primary schools should encourage, it is no less important. It is, after all, during the secondary school years that pupil disaffection is most likely to manifest itself in truancy, anti-social behaviour, educational under-performance and offending.

Effective schools are those which are less likely to marginalise disaffected pupils and more likely to have good, trusting relationships with parents. Many parents, however, are unaware of their importance to the process of secondary education. Seven out of ten parents in one survey believed that teachers were capable of teaching their children without their help while 66% of teachers disagreed with the proposition that they were capable of teaching the child without the parents' help.[58]

Teachers, meanwhile, often believe that a good relationship between parents and schools is more likely to be established through informal social contacts than formal consultative arrangements which tend to be dominated by middle class par-

ents of successful children.[59] Prospectuses, talks, open days, circulars and magazines and Parent Teacher Associations are among the methods used by schools to maintain home-school links, but these should be seen as means to reinforce personal contacts rather than replace them. Improving the relationship between schools and those parents not normally interested in education is one of the main aims behind the idea of community schools described below.

Homework policies

Another method of involving parents is through a homework policy. As Peter Mortimore observes:

"For parents, homework provides an opportunity, if not to look inside, at least to be aware of one aspect of school life. If they wish, parents are able, via the homework, to see what topics are being covered and at what level".[60]

Even when their knowledge of the particular subject is not great, parents can help by listening or testing when something has to be learned. It should be added that for some parents, homework provides a legitimate reason for keeping children off the streets.[61]

Some schools offer clear guidelines on the part parents can play in helping children with their homework. Non-attenders often turn out not to have a quiet place in their home to do their homework. In such cases, the school can provide rooms for homework to be done after school.[62]

Communicating with parents

Parent contact is easier when the school is accessible, familiar and welcoming. This is simpler to achieve with nursery, infant and junior schools. There are, nevertheless, examples of successful efforts to involve parents in their children's education at secondary level.[63] Since communication with parents at secondary school level is likely to be less frequent, it is important that what does occur is of a high quality. For example, parents prefer positive and personalised letters about their children rather than duplicated circulars.[64] The Inspectorate further suggests that the conditions for high attendance can be set when the school manages the induction of new pupils skilfully and explains policies to parents with care. In areas of ethnic diversity, schools have made extensive use of community languages and leaders in liaising with parents.

Most parents do not see home visiting as part of the secondary school teacher's job – although it can be effective when the school wants the parents' co-operation in encouraging a child to return to school after a period of absence.[65]

Community schools

Schools can be an important resource for the local community and thereby improve their relationships with parents. A number of authorities, such as Coventry, have recognised that both the intensive use of school buildings and community identification with schools can reduce vandalism. Some schools are officially designated as "community schools", others have developed a wide range of community activities over the years. The Schools Inspectorate suggests that some aspects of community schools may have positive effects on the behaviour of pupils, for example:

- *The commitment of the wider community to the aims of the school*

- *The presence of more adults on the premises*

- *The opportunity to involve pupils in helping the very young and the very old*

- *Opportunities for teachers and parents to meet informally*

- *An improved image for the school[66].*

It is particularly beneficial to develop a programme of community activities where particular attention is given to involving young people and parents whose interest in normal school activities is weak.[67]

This chapter has demonstrated that one of the most important ways in which schools can have a delinquency-reducing effect is through building a strong and trusting relationship with parents. Effective schools are a pre-condition for good relations between home and school since they are better able to motivate reluctant learners and develop the interest of parents in their children's education. Parental interest and heightened aspirations encourage further pupil success. Two important risk factors associated with anti-social behaviour, bullying and delinquency – parental disinterest and pupil failure in school – are thereby addressed.

The next chapter moves on to consider ways in which other community services can support families and reinforce the work of parents and schools in preventing offending and anti-social behaviour.

A note on the 1988 Education Reform Act

There are aspects of the government's reforms which may, unintentionally, operate against delinquency prevention efforts. For example, the requirement to publish "unweighted" examination league tables (which measure attainment rather than progress) creates a disincentive for schools to accommodate those young people who are most at risk of failing. These and other matters arising from recent legislation are discussed in Chapter 6.

1 National Children's Bureau (1990)

2 ibid

3 Reviewed in Rutter, M. and Madge, N. (1976)

4 For further details, see Bright, J. (1992)

5 In the order of 10-15 points. The best results have been achieved by those that emphasise language development.

6 Rutter, M. & Madge, N. (1976) and Ontario Ministry of Community and Social Services (1988)

7 Schweinhart, L.J. (1987) and Schweinhart, L.J. & Weikart, D.P. (1993). See Berrueta-Clement, J. et al (1984) for case histories

8 Schweinhart, L.J. & Weikart, D.P. (1993).

9 ibid and Lazar, I. & Darlington, R. (1982)

10 Schweinhart, L.J. et al (1986)

11 The average IQs of all three groups rose by 27 points in a year. ibid.

12 Lazar, I. & Darlington, R. (1982), also cited in Osborn, A.F. & Millbank, J.E. (1987)

13 Schweinhart, L.J. et al (1986)

14 See Woodhead, M. (1985) for discussion

15 Ministry of Community and Social Services, Ontario (1990)

16 Family Violence and Crime Reduction Projects funded by the Home Office Programme Development Unit. Commons Written Answer 26th June 1992

17 Schweinhart, L.J. (1987)

18 Woodhead, M. (1985)

19 Osborn, A.F. & Millbank, J.E. (1987)

20 Hayes, R.& Saunders, L.(1992)

21 Besharov, D. (1987)

22 See Osborn, A.F. & Millbank, J.E. (1986) for evidence that well-run playgroups provide some of the most educationally effective pre-school experience available

23 Cohen, B. (1990)

24 Jowett, S. & Sylva, K. (1986)

25 Schweinhart et al (1986)

26 Osborn, A.F. & Millbank, J.E. (1987)

27 ibid.

52

28 Woodhead, M. (1985)

29 Mortimore, P. (1991)

30 See Clarke, R. in Rutter, M. & Madge, N. (1976)

31 Jencks et al (1972)

32 See, for example, Rutter, M. et al (1979); Mortimore, P. (1988) and Smith, D. & Tomlinson, S. (1989)

33 Graham, J. (1988)

34 Rutter, M. et al (1979)

35 Mortimore, P. (1991)

36 ibid

37 Mortimore, P (1988)

38 Cauce, A.M. et al (1987); Comer, J.P. (1980a) and Comer, J.P. (1980b). But see also Farrington, D.P (1986) for a qualification of their view.

39 Quoted in Ontario Ministry of Community and Social Services (1990)

40 ibid

41 Douglas, J. (1964)

42 Quoted in Cyster et al (1979)

43 Mortimore, P. & Mortimore, J. (1984)

44 Cyster et al (1979) and Jowett, S. et al (1991)

45 Mortimore, J. & Mortimore, P. (1984)

46 Hannon, P. (1991)

47 ibid

48 ibid

49 Rutter, M. et al (1979)

50 ibid cited in Farrington, D.P. (1986)

51 Smith, D.J. & Tomlinson, S. (1989)

52 ibid

53 Graham, J. (1990)

54 ibid

55 ibid

56 Rutter, M. et al (1979)

57 Farrington, D.P. (1980) "Truancy, Delinquency, the Home and the School" in Hersor, L. & Berg, I. (eds) "Out of School: Modern Perspectives in Truancy and School Refusal" Chichester: Wiley pp 49–63

58 Lingard, A. & Allard, J. (1982)

59 ibid

60 Mortimore, P. & Mortimore, J. (1984)

61 Lingard, A. & Allard, J. (1982)

62 ibid

63 Her Majesty's Inspectorate of Schools(1989)

64 ibid

65 ibid

66 Her Majesty's Inspectorate of Schools(1987)

67 National Association for the Care and Resettlement of Offenders (1991)

68 Definition taken from Farrington, D.P. (1993)

69 ibid.

70 Especially their fathers. See Olweus, D. (1984)

71 Olweus, D. (1991)

72 Olweus, D. (1992)

73 Farrington, D.P. (1993)

74 ibid.

75 ibid.

76 Crime Concern (1992)

77 Roland, E. (1989)

78 Olweus, D. (1990) and (1991)

79 Farrington, D.P. (1993)

80 ibid. reporting additional data supplied by Richard Tremblay. Main study described in Tremblay et al (1991) and (1992)

Families and the community

"Juvenile crime prevention is something for the whole community to tackle together." Report of the Home Office Standing Conference on Crime Prevention's working group on Juvenile Crime.[1]

The preceding chapters have considered services delivered directly to families and examined the ways that schools can support families and help inhibit delinquency. If the benefits of social crime prevention are to be maximised, however, a third ingredient is necessary. This relates to whether particular neighbourhoods make it easier or more difficult for families to supervise their children and exercise responsibility in the way that they would like. Poorly-managed council estates built in a maze of walkways without adequate play areas, for example, create a handicap for even the best-motivated parents.[2] Conversely, the benefits of investing in parent education programmes and quality pre-school education are likely to be enhanced if the children's physical environment is well designed and intelligently managed. Children and their parents can derive values and attitudes from the communities in which they live. A sensible strategy for preventing youth crime will make sure that neighbourhoods as well as families are targeted.

In this chapter, the term *design* refers both to the external layout of a neighbourhood or estate ("environmental design") and to the type of buildings ("building design"). It is usually talked about in the context of particular local authority housing estates whose shortcomings are thought to exacerbate crime problems. *Neighbourhood management* is concerned with the assessment of residents' needs, the provision of community services, the participation of local residents and the co-ordination of activity by various agencies. The concept extends beyond the management of particular services and can apply to neighbourhoods where private and public housing are mixed and to estates managed by local authorities or housing associations.

Well-designed and well-managed neighbourhoods support families because they create a context in which the supervision of children can be undertaken more easily. Informal controls arise naturally to check anti-social and criminal behaviour so that young people quickly learn what they can and cannot do. In areas where informal controls are weak, parents find it much more difficult to exercise control over their young because their efforts are not reinforced by the wider community.

The consequences for families under stress can be very serious. If there is no effective supervision either inside or outside the home, children are at much greater risk of harming themselves, drifting into delinquency and being taken into care. In communities where there are disproportionate numbers of such families, it is doubly important to strengthen informal community controls. Evidence from regeneration schemes on particularly run-down estates shows that a small number of marginalised, anti-social families can pose a serious threat to order and stability in already vulnerable communities.[3]

It is at the neighbourhood level, too, that social prevention and "situational" crime prevention – making crime harder to commit – come together. Programmes that support the family are most likely to be successful if they are complemented by measures aimed at reducing opportunities for crime and anti-social behaviour. Both are necessary and both should have their place in an overall community crime prevention strategy.

Security and design

It is argued by some that well-designed residential areas are able to reduce crime *and* the likelihood of children and young people drifting into delinquency.[4] Good design, it is claimed, not only makes it easier for residents to supervise children but also stimulates community confidence and strengthens informal controls on children's behaviour. Their surroundings make them less inclined to misbehave and offend. The ideal type of residential neighbourhood is considered to be one composed of traditional streetscapes with families living in conventional houses with gardens.[5]

Remedial design work commonly applied to housing estates includes the provision of front and rear gardens and reductions in the amount of undesignated open space around them since this is often misused and considered unsafe. Other changes include improvements to lighting, road and pedestrian access and improving sightlines. Estates of a complex, non-traditional, design often require major structural changes like the removal of walkways or the installation of entryphone systems or concierges on duty at entrances. The aim is to improve natural surveillance, to make the estate less accessible to prowlers and to create "defensible space" around individual properties.[6]

55

The notion that design can reduce crime is supported, to some extent, by research. However, the evidence suggests that design is not always the most important factor associated with high crime rates.[7] There are estates composed of conventional houses and streets which have high crime rates and some tower block estates which have low crime rates. Much depends on who lives in the estates and how the estates are managed.

The extent of social disadvantage among residents and the proportion of children to adults on an estate are more significant factors influencing crime rates.[8] Housing managers can, in some cases, influence these factors by adjusting the match between the design of an estate and the types of household that are allocated accommodation. High child densities, for example, are invariably associated with vandalism and the problem is intensified if large numbers of children are housed within multi-storey blocks.[9] Unfortunately, local authorities in some cities have no alternative to housing families in such blocks because Right To Buy legislation has diminished their stock of houses and they are unable to replace them. But even in these circumstances, preventive measures can be adopted. One authority houses homeless families in a tower block, but has allocated a whole floor for childcare and pre-school provision.

The style of management is also important: communal housing in blocks of flats demands a more intensive style of management than estates of houses. The localised management style pioneered by the Priority Estates Project in partnership with local authorities emphasises tenant involvement, local control over budgets, services and allocations and the presence of caretakers, community wardens and concierges to create a well-ordered environment.[10]

Neighbourhood management

Tackling crime in many areas requires a broader and more rigorous approach than is commonly found. This can be achieved through a process of neighbourhood management by which the needs of an area are thoroughly assessed and a programme of multi-agency action implemented with the involvement of local people. Good neighbourhood management should help prevent both crime and incivilities such as drunkenness, hooliganism, harassment, disorderly and threatening behaviour, abandoned cars, fly-tipping, vandalism and graffiti. In many areas, these are more of a problem than 'real' crime because they are more commonplace and visible. Left unchecked, they generate fear and create the sort of disorderly, uncared-for environment which attracts offenders and causes individuals and businesses to leave. The result is a

spiral of decline from which it can be very difficult for a neighbourhood to recover.[11]

Neighbourhood management can be sub-divided into four headings:

- *Service provision*
- *Community policing*
- *Provision for children and young people*
- *Community involvement.*

Service provision

Neighbourhoods, particularly those characterised by a high proportion of council or housing association stock, are dependent on a wide range of services. The quality of life can be improved substantially if such services are delivered effectively and responsively. Housing management and repairs, discussed above, figure large among them. But there are also social services, recreation and youth, policing and cleansing and refuse as well as local voluntary services. In many areas, services have been decentralised to improve their quality and fill gaps in provision.

Community policing

The emphasis in this study on the crime prevention role of agencies outside the criminal justice system does not mean there is no role for the police. Community policing is an essential part of any community safety strategy. The most promising models involve police forming partnerships with local communities and assigning officers to permanent neighbourhood beats.

In parts of the United States, officers have sought to address the root causes of crime and disorder by working very closely with other agencies and with the community itself.[12] Unfortunately, this rigorous approach to community policing is not commonly found in Britain. It would require officers to be assigned to areas for 2-3 years and ensure consistency of policing style as well as personnel. Police would come to know many of the young people in their beat who were most at risk of offending. This is crucial if relationships are to be built up and prevention projects given time to work.

Such policing does not require the resurrection of a "Dixon of Dock Green" style long since gone. Nor is it the same as existing "home beat" policing which in many areas commands low priority from police managers and is seen as unplanned, undirected and not very effective by local residents.[13] It calls for a more sophisticated approach already at the cutting edge of policing in some American cities and in a few places in Britain

56

where forces are making a real contribution to creating safe and orderly neighbourhoods.

Provision for children and young people

The aim should be to provide adequate mainstream recreation activities as well as specific facilities targeted at young people at risk of delinquency. Despite a shortage of supporting research evidence,[14] there is widespread support for the notion that recreation programmes for young people can engage their interest in constructive activities, making it less likely they will drift into offending. However, only a minority of young people currently use Youth Service provision (probably much less than 30% in most areas[15]) and few youth work programmes have delinquency prevention as one of their stated objectives.[16]

John Graham and Douglas Smith, in a recent report, have suggested that the Youth Service, by concentrating its resources on specific groups of young people in areas with high rates of juvenile offending, could make a significant contribution to a community-based strategy for diverting young people away from crime. They lay particular emphasis on the need for "detached" youth workers to make contact with young people in the places where they naturally congregate and provide a bridge with the local agencies that can best meet their needs.[17]

It is clear that a sharper focus is required as well as different strategies targeted at different groups. For example:

- Organised clubs and activities are best for under-14s, but in many areas the youth service does not cater for younger children

- Older young people respond better to a drop-in resource centre approach which encourages them to take responsibility for their own activities, including adult-style clubs, serving non-alcoholic drinks

- Outreach or detached youth work aimed at contacting and involving young people most at risk of offending is needed

- Young people are often at loggerheads with their parents, teachers and other adults. A youth counselling or mediation programme can provide them with the support they are otherwise unable or unwilling to seek.

Among the preventive projects which have been developed in the community for school age children are:

- *Summer holiday activity schemes*
- *Youth clubs and childrens' centres*
- *Adventure playgrounds*
- *After school clubs*

Action for older Young People (16-25) includes:

- *Drop-in centres*
- *Outreach/detached youth work*
- *Young adult centres*
- *Youth mediation schemes*
- *Peer-led drug prevention*
- *Advice and counselling*
- *Motor mechanics and learning to drive*

Community involvement

Finally, there is the contribution local residents themselves can make to improving the quality of life in their neighbourhoods and supporting each other in raising and supervising children. Residents, for example, have increasingly important roles to play in the management of schools in their role as school governors. They can set up playgroups and youth activities where they may serve as volunteers and on management committees. They may be involved in efforts to regenerate local economies. They can campaign for, and contribute to, design changes to their estates and be involved to a greater or lesser degree in their management. They may also be concerned with providing direct services through residents' associations, mediation schemes, play and youth projects, victim support and Neighbourhood Watch.

There is an increasing bank of knowledge on good practice and on the types of community involvement that are most effective and sustainable. It is, moreover, unlikely that much of the social and recreational provision considered desirable for neighbourhood crime prevention would be viable without a significant input from volunteers.

There are, however, two pre-conditions for maximising the voluntary involvement of local residents:

- The first is an effective response by the statutory agencies to neighbourhood problems that they alone have the authority and resources to tackle. The most important of these agencies are the police and the local authority. The fact that some tasks are beyond the capabilities of volunteers is not always recognised. The result is that some community crime prevention initiatives have been over-dependent on voluntary effort. Those who become involved can rapidly become despondent when faced with problems they cannot hope to tackle.

57

- The second is an adequate system for recruiting and supporting volunteers. Volunteers need not only come from the immediate locality and a system has to be in place for assessing, training and placing them. Local young people should be encouraged to participate as volunteer youth and community workers. Emphasis should also be placed on involving unemployed people. Skill audits can identify a wide range of local commitment and expertise that might otherwise go unused.

Statutory and voluntary agencies should, meanwhile, create the context in which local voluntary effort is most likely to flourish. To do this, additional support is needed from government such as that already provided by the Department of Health's *Opportunities For Volunteering Fund*. This is a limited but excellent source which recognises that voluntary activity cannot thrive without support in the form of paid organisers and resources for equipment and transport.

Grants from funds like this generate many times their value in terms of volunteer labour and additional resources from fundraising efforts. Much of this voluntary activity provides facilities for families, children and young people.[19] *In so doing, it strengthens communities and makes a significant contribution to supervising young people and diverting them from offending.*[20]

13 National Association for the Care and Resettlement of Offenders (1988)

14 See Graham, J. & Smith, D.I. (1993)

15 Graham, J. & Smith, D.I. (1993)

16 Gill, K. (1992)

17 Graham, J. & Smith, D.I. (1993)

18 A distinction, however, needs to be drawn between initiatives which are available to all young people (such as adventure playgrounds or youth clubs) and those where efforts are made to target those considered to be especially "at risk" of offending young people (such as some holiday play schemes).A third category covers Intermediate Treatment schemes and other rehabilitation projects to which young people are referred by the courts, police or social services.

19 See Knight, B. & Osborn, S. (1992)

20 National Association for the Care and Resettlement of Offenders (1991)

1 Home Office Standing conference on Crime Prevention (1987)

2 Harriett Wilson's work in the West Midlands confirms the difficulties parents encounter in trying to supervise their children when there is no proper play provision Wilson, H. (1980)

3 Power, A. (1986)

4 See, notably, Coleman, A. (1987)

5 ibid

6 Dept. of the Environment (1991)

7 Newman, O. (1980)

8 ibid. See also, Page, D. (1993) for evidence that housing management mistakes of the 1960s and 1970s are being repeated by housing associations.

9 Dept.of the Environment (1981) and Home Office (1979)

10 Power, A. (1986)

11 Skogan, W. (1990)

12 Trojanowicz, R. & Bucqueroux, B. (1990)

CHAPTER 6

Legislation, crime and the family

"It shall be the general duty of every local authority...a) to safeguard and promote the welfare of children within their area who are in need; and b) so far as is consistent with that duty, to promote the upbringing of such children by their families, by providing a range and level of services appropriate to those children's needs." Children Act 1989: Part III, Section 17,i.

Increasing recognition of the potential role of the family in preventing delinquency and crime is reflected in recent legislation. The Children Act 1989, the Criminal Justice Act 1991 and the Child Support Act 1991 all, in varying degrees, aspire to providing better support for families or, in the case of the two latter pieces of legislation, to enforcing responsibilities on parents. The 1988 Education Reform Act and subsequent 1992 Education White Paper and Bill also have important implications for future efforts to tackle truancy and delinquency. This chapter reviews these and other changes in the law that may help or hinder progress towards better social prevention of crime.

Children Act 1989

Family services

The Children Act places a duty on local authorities to safeguard and promote the welfare of children within their area who are in need. Consistent with that duty they are also required to assist the upbringing of these children by their families by providing a range of appropriate family support services. Children's needs have to be assessed according to their age, sex, religion, culture and language. Children in need are defined as those who are unlikely to achieve, maintain or have the opportunity of achieving a reasonable standard of physical, intellectual, emotional, social or behavioural development.

As seen in Chapter 3, the Act places a further duty on local authorities to review and report on the childcare services in their area used by children under 8. These reviews are intended to improve co-ordination and standards of service as well as the spread of childcare facilities.

Guidance and Regulations accompanying the Children Act stress the importance of co-ordinating early childhood facilities in order to give maximum benefit to the community.[1] They suggest that local authorities develop inter-departmental strategies for supporting children and their families.

Family centres offering both therapeutic and community services are recommended under a general duty within the Act. Other services proposed include volunteer based befriending schemes such as those provided by Home Start and Newpin, drop-in centres, parent-toddler groups, play buses, play groups, day nurseries, supported child minding, out-of-school clubs, holiday schemes and other supervised activities for children and young people. The co-ordination of child minding with nurseries and play groups is advised to give children the benefit of group activities. Provision of pre-school education facilities within day nurseries is also proposed to give children an intellectually stimulating environment. The Guidance emphasises the need to cater for the cultural, linguistic and other specific needs of children from different ethnic backgrounds.

The Children Act also places local authorities under a specific duty to prevent crime by measures that discourage juveniles from committing offences. The Guidance suggests that in addition to intermediate treatment for those at risk of offending and the supervision of juvenile offenders, this might involve advice and support services for parents.[2] The relevance of family support systems to delinquency prevention is thus, in a modest way, acknowledged.

Whether local authorities will have the inclination or resources to provide such services is, however, another matter. Concern has been expressed by a number of councils that they will have difficulties meeting their obligation to families laid down in the Act because of inadequate funding.[3]

The Act is not prescriptive, requiring authorities to set the level of services they consider appropriate for the children in their area. The definition of children "in need" is open to varying interpretations and could be construed quite narrowly. There is already some evidence that local authorities do not see their duty to assist children in need as directly connected to their responsibility under the Act for preventing delinquency.[4] This will inevitably limit the scope of their responses.

Parental responsibility

The focus of the Children Act is on the needs of children and the legislation lays stress on the

61

The Criminal Justice Act 1991

Ministers, in the late 1980s, spoke with increasing fervour of the need for parents to be held to account for their children's criminal actions. Their view was reflected in the 1991 Criminal Justice Act which requires parents of young people accused of criminal offences to attend court with their child. Sentencers are given sanctions to enforce their attendance unless this would be "unreasonable". The law also makes parents responsible for any financial penalties imposed on children under 16 unless that, too, would be unreasonable. The courts can, moreover, bind parents over so that they face a financial penalty of up to £1,000 if they fail to exercise sufficient care and control of their children in future.

Margaret Shaw, in her review of criminal justice legislation, has shown that this political concern to promote the responsibility of parents is not new.[5] The Children and Young Persons Act 1933, for example, allowed magistrates to impose fines, damages or costs on the fathers or mothers of juvenile offenders where they considered the parents had failed in their responsibility to prevent misbehaviour. Hermann Mannheim commented on these powers in the 1940s that little use was made of them because they were regarded as unhelpful.[6] He quoted a report on delinquency in Bradford which suggested that the fining of parents undermined the relationship with their child. He added that a more useful approach would be to offer active support to parents in addressing problems with child-rearing.

Shaw reports that during the 1950s and 1960s relatively little use was made by the courts of their powers vis-a-vis parents and generally there was greater emphasis on the promotion of a welfare approach towards juvenile offending. In a review of juvenile legislation in Scotland, the 1964 Kilbrandon report[7] strongly opposed the imposition of penalties on parents by the courts: *"If relationships are already strained, to order a parent to pay a fine could make matters worse, leading, for example, to excessive physical punishment, or even to rejection from home, thus placing the youngster at more risk than ever"*.[8]

Punishment of parents has never been introduced in Scotland. In England and Wales, however, the 1982 Criminal Justice Act ammended and updated a number of parental coercion measures that were later reinforced by the 1991 Act.

The punishment model reflects an assumption that parents are indifferent to their children's offending behaviour and that they make no attempt to deal with it. This belief is not, however, supported by attitudinal research. For example, a study of parents of young offenders in Sheffield found that they already felt the pressure of responsibility for their children's behaviour, including a sense of being "on trial" themselves: *"They feel embarrassed and ashamed when the police keep coming to their homes to interview their children; they feel harassed or angry or upset when the police regularly insist on them coming to the police station when their children are interviewed. They face stigma from relatives, neighbours and friends."*[9]

It seems, therefore, that the effect of the coercive approach in the 1991 Act could be to exacerbate already difficult relations between parents and adolescents. It could also increase family tensions and lead to a higher incidence of family break-up. The evidence reviewed in the first two chapters of this book suggests that this will do nothing to assist efforts to reduce offending behaviour among young people.

---

responsibility of parents to meet them. This emphasis is reflected in the Act's curtailment of the power of local authorities to intervene in family life. The local authority's role is defined in terms of supporting parents and enabling them to fulfil their responsibilities for children, instead of removing responsibility from them. There is a specific duty placed on councils to divert young people from prosecution. Care orders can no longer be imposed by courts in criminal proceedings and the fact that a young person has committed offences is no longer one of the accepted criteria for bringing care proceedings.

The sole grounds for care orders now relate to the welfare of the child. Young people must be deemed to be suffering significant harm (or likely to suffer such harm) either because they are beyond parental control or because they are suffering from an unreasonably low standard of care.

The removal of a child into the care of the local authority is, hence, no longer considered an appropriate way of preventing delinquency. It is still possible for a juvenile offender whose home circumstances are thought to contribute to offending to be placed in local authority accommodation for up to six months. But this can only be done as an addition to a supervision order, and it does not remove the parents' responsibility for the young person concerned.

The Children Act also seeks to legislate against truancy by reinforcing parents' responsibility to ensure school attendance. They are formally required to comply with any directions given under an education supervision order that arises from their children's failure to attend school.

The Child Support Act 1991

Against the background of rising levels of lone parenthood and associated poverty – with serious implications for juvenile delinquency – the government has legislated to make more absent parents pay maintenance for their children. Since 70 per cent of lone mothers[10] at any one time are receiving Income Support, the effect of the new regime on child poverty is likely to be limited. This is because any maintenance payments are deducted from benefit on a pound for pound basis. A maintenance "disregard" of £15 on Family Credit payments made to lone parents who work for low pay may, however, leave some families less thoroughly trapped on the "poverty plateau".[11]

The Act also threatens lone parents who refuse to co-operate in the pursuit of maintenance with deductions from their personal allowance within Income Support. They will only be excused if they believe that they or their children would suffer "harm or significant distress" by revealing the absent parent's name and whereabouts. The way in which the exemption is interpreted is likely to prove crucial.[12]

Possible problems have also been envisaged for the children of second families. Parents have a financial responsibility for all their children, but the formula for assessing parental maintenance obligations towards the children of an earlier relationship has been attacked as inflexible and for not taking sufficient account of their financial commitments to any children from a current relationship.[13] The welfare of children in second families may, therefore, be placed under stress.

Education Reform Act 1988

The Government has recently made significant changes to what this report has treated as an "extended arm" of the family; namely the schools system. The introduction of the Education Reform Act 1988 has introduced a national curriculum and local management of schools. The former is intended to ensure higher academic standards. The latter transfers major aspects of school management from local education authorities to headteachers and school governing bodies with the declared intention of increasing parental choice.

Viewed optimistically, the re-organisation of education in this way presents an opportunity for schools to contribute to delinquency prevention through new management arrangements and teaching methods. In practice, features of the new educational philosophy and structures could actually inhibit the ability of schools to prevent crime.

The National Curriculum

Under the National Curriculum, foundation subjects – including three core subjects – take up most of the timetable. Those subjects which belong to the broader developmental role of the school, such as personal and social education, are required but have mainly to be covered within the foundation subjects.[14] Doubts have been expressed as to whether some aspects of personal and social education relevant to crime prevention – for example, sensible attitudes to alcohol – will be dealt with adequately.[15]

Given the links between underachievement in school and delinquency, there are also concerns over the academic focus of the curriculum and the problems it implies for less able children. A survey of 38,000 pupils on truancy found that many average and low ability pupils are having problems with GCSE coursework and are consequently absent from classes.[16] Another study suggests that three out of four pupils whose attainment is low already fail to get the help they need at school by the time they reach 14.[17] The authors express concern over politically-inspired demands for a return to more "traditional" teaching values and the pressure placed on schools to demonstrate examination success. This trend was seen as undermining innovative attempts to assist underachievers such as the Low Achieving Pupils Programme (LAPP).[18]

Local management of schools

The devolved management of schools and the provision for some to "opt out" of local authority control will have considerable impact on the development of youth crime prevention strategies. Schools face upheaval in taking on a local management role and there is a danger that the wider social responsibilities of schools will be forced by administrative pressure to assume a lower priority.

A competitive market has been introduced into education with schools being partly funded on the basis of the number of pupils they can attract. This and the publication of examination league tables is inevitably encouraging some headteachers to focus their efforts on achieving demonstrable academic success rather than devoting resources to children who are low achievers or disruptive. Enactment of the Education Bill will increase competitiveness between schools, as well as encouraging many more "opt-outs" from local authority control to grant-maintained status.

The 1989 Annual Report of HM Senior Chief Inspector of Schools, meanwhile, judged 30% of the lessons surveyed as poor or very poor and commented that:

63

"Sadly, less able pupils are much more likely to experience the poor and shoddy than the more able: a worryingly persistent feature of English education at all levels."

Exclusions from school

There is, in particular, disturbing evidence of a serious rise in the number of young people who are being excluded from schools. The desire of head teachers to rid themselves of "nuisance" children has been attributed, in part, to the new environment created by the reform process. A survey conducted by the National Union of Teachers (NUT) shows that school exclusions rose by 20 per cent in the academic year 1990/91.[19] But a BBC Panorama/MORI survey covering the two years ending July 1992 suggests a 50 per cent increase, with as many as 66,000 pupils – or 1 per cent of schoolchildren – being excluded each year. Although 8 per cent of education authorities thought poorer pupil discipline was to blame, 42% cited competition between schools arising from the 1988 reforms and another 22 per cent the pressure which the reforms had placed on timetables.[20] The Department for Education's own figures covering those exclusions described as "permanent" reveal much smaller numbers, but a significant increase from 2,910 in 1990-91 to 3,833 in 1991-2.[21]

The risk is that a system may emerge where children from advantaged homes are educated in "popular" grant-maintained schools while "problem" children are left behind in the remnants of LEA schools. Educational research over the past thirty years suggests that this could lead to resentment and disaffection and a net increase in levels of anti-social behaviour and delinquency.

The government's 1992 Education White Paper seeks to counteract this danger by proposing a power for Local Education Authorities to require grant-maintained and LEA schools to accept specified pupils who would otherwise be without a place. Consideration is also being given to financial incentives, or disincentives, for schools to reduce the number of exclusions. The workings of the 1986 Education (No 2) Act which sets out head teachers' powers of exclusion are being reviewed.[22]

Support services

The 1992 Education White Paper proposes that local education authorities should continue to be responsible for welfare support services to schools such as the education social work service and the education psychological service which play an important part in helping schools to cope with behavioural and delinquency problems.[23] Local authorities are also to be placed under a duty to provide an education service outside the school setting for children who need it.

The continuing role of local authorities as providers of educational support services has been welcomed as a way of achieving a co-ordinated service with sufficient expertise. There are, however, concerns that schools may be expected to pay for any support they receive from locally managed budgets and that school welfare services will continue to be under-resourced. The Elton Report on "Discipline in Schools" stressed the difficulties caused by an over-stretched education psychological service which was unable to assess children with special educational needs quickly enough.[24]

Community use of schools

It is generally recognised that the community use of schools can help to improve the social education of pupils and that it has the potential to prevent delinquency. Prior to the introduction of local management, education authorities could subsidise schools to encourage community use. The DES Circular 16/10/89, "The Use of School Premises for Childcare Provision out of School Hours", which followed the Education Reform Act, encourages such use of schools, but then appears to curtail any subsidy: *"LEAs and governing bodies will need to bear in mind that under Local Management of Schools the schools budget may not subsidise any non-school use of its premises."*[25]

A number of education authorities have been able to maintain the community use of schools by identifying funds outside the central funding formula. Others have developed the outside use of the schools on business principles where the costs incurred are covered by the lettings charge. This approach, however, works against community groups in deprived areas who may have difficulty raising the necessary cash.[27]

Local Education Authorities

Another inevitable consequence of the reforms is that the role of local education authorities in co-ordinating a youth crime prevention strategy will be diminished. They will be less able to give a lead in developing the kind of school management practices described in Chapter 4 which might contribute to the prevention of delinquency. The substantially reduced role of local education authorities envisaged by the Education White Paper also seems likely to create difficulties for council departments trying to work together to promote the welfare of children as required by the Children Act. There are further concerns that the provision for regular reviews of childcare, with co-ordination across education, social services, the voluntary and the private sectors is being undermined by the increasing autonomy being granted to schools. The Education Reform Act has also failed to support local authorities in the provision of nursery education.[27]

With the very limited policy development role now left to local education authorities, consideration needs to be given to ways of co-ordinating and promoting educational practices which might contribute to the prevention of delinquency.

Conflicts of interest

There appears, in summary, to be a mismatch among the various items of recent legislation which could undermine the capacity of central and local government to assist stressed and disadvantaged families whose children are at risk of delinquency. The "punitive" approach to enforcing parental responsibility adopted in the Criminal Justice Act and the Child Support Act sends out confusing signals and risks undermining the "supportive" approach towards families envisaged under the Children Act. Similarly, the reduced strategic role of local education authorities envisaged by the Education Reform Act appears in conflict with the Children Act by making it more difficult for councils to co-ordinate and promote services for children in their area.

A more consistent philosophy is required if family policies are to be adopted that are capable of contributing towards the prevention of delinquency. What such far-reaching policies might look like is the subject of the concluding chapter.

1   The Children Act 1989. Guidance Regulations Vol 2. *Family Support, day Care and Educational Provision for Young Children* (1991) HMSO

2   ibid.

3   Fox Harding (1991)

4   National Association for the Care and Resettlement of Offenders (1993)

5   Shaw, M. (1986)

6   Mannheim, H. (1948)

7   Kilbrandon Report (1964)

8   ibid.

9   National Association for the Care and Resettlement of Offenders (1992)

10 Bradshaw, J. and Millar, J. (1991) Nine out of ten lone parents are women. See Burghes, L. (1993a)

11 Burghes, L. (1993a)

12 Burghes, L (1991) and (1993a)

13 Save the Children (1992) unpublished briefing

14 Dept. of Education and Science (1989)

15 See, for example, Home Office Standing Committee on Crime Prevention (1987b)

16 O'Keefe, D. and Stoll, P. (1992) Polytechnic of North London. Cited in Sunday Express 31-5-1992

17 Stradling, R., Saunders, L and Weston, P. (1992)

18 ibid.

19 National Union of Teachers. Survey on Pupils' Exclusions; information from LEAs. (May 1992)

20 MORI/BBC Panorama (1993)

21 Returns from National Exclusions Reporting System. Department for Education

22 Dept. for Education (1992)

23 Dept. for Education/Welsh Office (1992)

24 Dept. of Education and Science/Welsh Office (1989)

25 Dept. of Education and Science (1989)

26 National Association for the Care and Resettlement of Offenders 1991

27 Pugh, G. (1992)

CHAPTER 7

Conclusions: an agenda for prevention

"We are all victims of crime. Those who have not themselves been attacked or had their possessions stolen or damaged, bear their share of the costs of dealing with offenders and of taking preventive measures." Report to the Home Office Standing Conference on Crime Prevention.[1]

The costs of crime, in terms of human distress and wasted resources, are enormous. A Home Office working party which examined the financial implications – stolen and damaged property, medical care, injuries compensation, policing, the courts, probation and prisons – concluded that many thousands of millions of pounds are involved each year.[2] Unofficially, the quantifiable figures were thought by the working party to be comparable to the costs of running the entire National Health Service (£18bn in 1988).[3] Shops are believed to lose at least £2bn a year through pilfering, while annual losses to individuals and families through theft have been estimated at another £2 billion.[4] But that takes no account of either the personal misery of victims nor the fear of crime which cuts even deeper into society. The television pictures of mass vandalism and disorder connected with so-called "joy riding" in the summer of 1991 demonstrated vividly how whole communities can become the victims of crime.

The cost of administering the criminal justice system in England and Wales – police, courts, probation and prisons – was alone more than £9 billion in 1992-3 – a 100 per cent increase since 1978-9[5] (**Table 1**). Yet the majority of crimes are never reported to police[6] and only a small minority of those are ever, in any sense, "solved". Despite such vast public expense, crime surveys suggest that just 3 per cent of offences result in a known perpetrator being cautioned or prosecuted[7] (**Tables 2 and 3**).

This report has been about tackling crime by attacking its roots – including the nine out of ten offences that are never cleared up by the criminal justice system. Its conclusions are based on a premise that far from being unable to afford new initiatives, policy makers can no longer afford **not** to act. Moreover, the very substantial slice of soaring crime costs that is attributable to young offenders must contradict any argument that young delinquents can safely be left to "grow out" of crime on their own.[8]

The high cost of crime supports the case for **deterrence** through the police and criminal justice system. The odds that offenders will be caught and punished need to be increased. It endorses the continuing good sense of action to **reduce the**

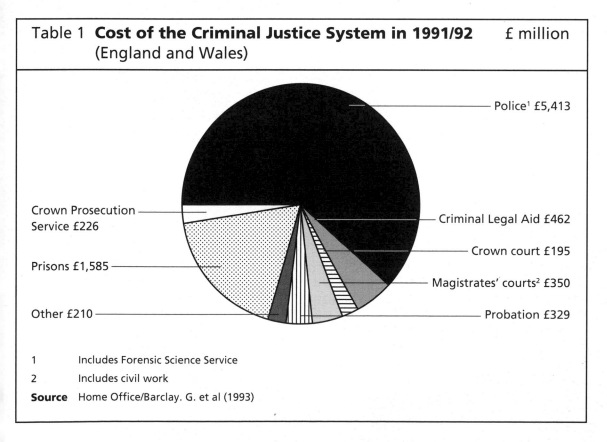

Table 1 **Cost of the Criminal Justice System in 1991/92** £ million (England and Wales)

- Police[1] £5,413
- Criminal Legal Aid £462
- Crown court £195
- Magistrates' courts[2] £350
- Probation £329
- Other £210
- Prisons £1,585
- Crown Prosecution Service £226

1   Includes Forensic Science Service

2   Includes civil work

Source   Home Office/Barclay. G. et al (1993)

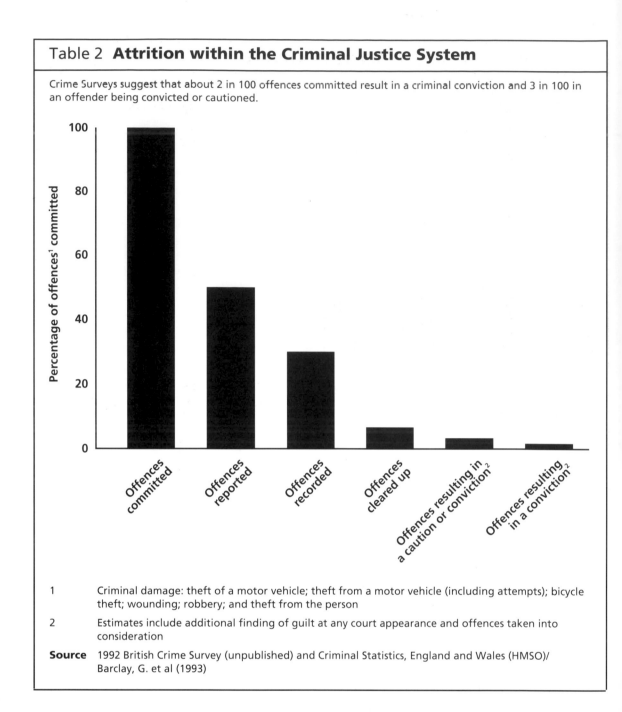

Table 2 **Attrition within the Criminal Justice System**

Crime Surveys suggest that about 2 in 100 offences committed result in a criminal conviction and 3 in 100 in an offender being convicted or cautioned.

1   Criminal damage: theft of a motor vehicle; theft from a motor vehicle (including attempts); bicycle theft; wounding; robbery; and theft from the person

2   Estimates include additional finding of guilt at any court appearance and offences taken into consideration

Source   1992 British Crime Survey (unpublished) and Criminal Statistics, England and Wales (HMSO)/ Barclay, G. et al (1993)

opportunities for crime. But it also makes the case for investment in a third, innovative strand of **social crime prevention** whose aim must be to prevent children from drifting into crime and to stop minor offenders turning into persistent, adult criminals. Support for families in the difficult task of child-rearing will be central to such a strategy.

A different approach

This study began by reviewing the research in Europe and the United States that has tried to identify the family circumstances most likely to produce delinquent children. The evidence suggests that the relationship between parent and child is the mechanism that determines whether tendencies towards aggressive and anti-social behaviour are inhibited or allowed to develop. Pov-

erty and other external stresses make it more difficult for parents to nurture their children with adequate affection, encouragement, discipline or supervision. But it is their style of parenting that exerts a direct influence over their children. The American criminologist, Travis Hirschi, in an influential study, characterised the nature of the developing parent-child relationship as a *"bond of affection"* whose strength can later determine the degree of resistance to breaking the law: *"The important consideration is whether the parent is psychologically present when temptation to a crime appears".*[9]

Indications that the influence of social or environmental pressures on children may be largely mediated through parenting behaviour[10] do not, however, imply that a prevention strategy need only

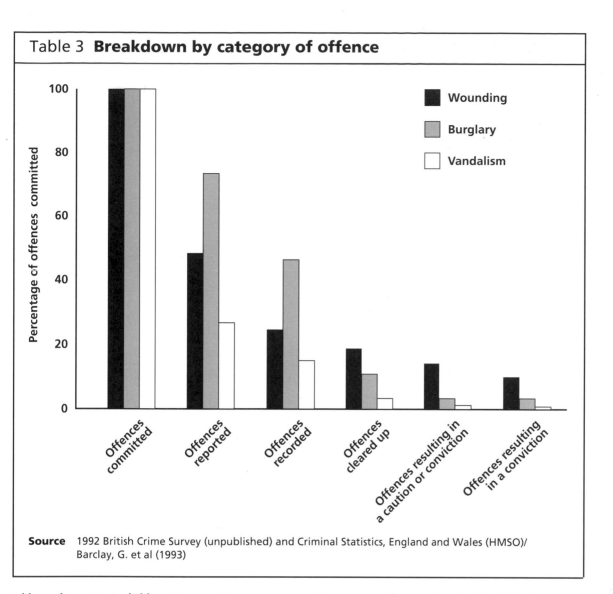

Table 3 **Breakdown by category of offence**

Legend:
- Wounding (black)
- Burglary (grey)
- Vandalism (white)

Y-axis: Percentage of offences committed

Categories: Offences committed, Offences reported, Offences recorded, Offences cleared up, Offences resulting in a caution or conviction, Offences resulting in a conviction

Source 1992 British Crime Survey (unpublished) and Criminal Statistics, England and Wales (HMSO)/ Barclay, G. et al (1993)

address the nation's child-rearing practices to succeed. Nor would it be productive to portray such a programme as an exercise in "blaming" inadequate parents for crime. Some parents undoubtedly are neglectful and irresponsible, but there are few who are ever anything but dismayed to discover that their sons or daughters are in trouble with the law – including those who have criminal records themselves.[11] Contrary to theories about a workshy, inherently anti-social "underclass" appearing in Britain,[12] there is strong evidence that impoverished parents are at least as "pro-work" and "pro-children" as anyone else.[13] They may, however, lack the knowledge, skills and self-confidence that would make them effective parents when their children are young. They may also be living their lives in the face of daily adversity that saps their energies and ability to cope. As Gerald Patterson, Director of the Oregon Social Learning Center, puts it:

"Who do you blame for unemployment, mental depression or the other kinds of social disadvantage that interrupt your skills as a parent?".[14]

Parents struggling to raise their families in poverty and isolation on badly designed housing estates might well benefit from new ways of listening to children or exerting consistent discipline. But their interest in learning and their ability to apply new parenting skills is bound to be limited if the external pressures remain unchanged. Since the risks of delinquency are often greatest in families where clusters of adverse social factors occur,[15] it is evident that an effective prevention strategy will need to target several factors at once. Claims that criminality is entirely rooted in the pathology of individual families are as sterile as suggestions that poverty alone causes crime. Multiple problems, to borrow another phrase from the United States, demand multiple solutions.[16]

Family poverty and disadvantage

David Farrington and Donald West in their latest report on the Cambridge Study in Delinquent Development[17] suggest that the starting place for experiments in social crime prevention should be the targeting of three important predictors of offending: **poor parental child-rearing behaviour,** school failure and economic deprivation. Any general alleviation of poverty would, however, require detailed recommendations for the reform of the social security system which lie outside the scope of this paper. A recent study by Louie Burghes of options for improving the incomes of one parent families demonstrates the desirability of removing over two million children from dependence on Income Support, but it also exposes the complex interactions of the tax and benefit systems that would need to be unravelled and reconstituted.[18] The connections between family poverty and criminality are, nevertheless, persuasive evidence that the government should strive harder to raise the living standards of families with dependent children and to remove the "poverty traps" which inhibit self-sufficiency through earnings. As Gillian Pugh and Erica De'Ath wrote in their report on parent education:

> "Policies are needed that will enable all families to enjoy a basic level of income, commensurate with what is acceptable within a developed society, that will give them some genuine choice in how they live their lives and bring up their children."[19]

One important step in the right direction would be the wider availability of affordable and accessible childcare – making it worthwhile for parents to escape from the "safety net" of Income Support. Chapter 3 of this report highlights the current paucity of child care in the context of family poverty, but also its potential role in alleviating educational failure. Community nurseries, as operated by Strathclyde Regional Council and a number of English authorities, are combining day care with nursery education in a way that could provide a model for others to follow.

Family centres and other neighbourhood projects – especially those with an "open door" policy – seek to alleviate poverty and the associated stress on parents through a wide range of activities, including family outings, social events and such services as money advice, credit unions, thrift shops and toy libraries. Family preservation schemes, notably Home-Start, also help families to budget more effectively. This is all part of the argument for encouraging and expanding their prevention work – although, sadly, also a plea to preserve existing provision from cutbacks. As the Association of Chief Police Officers and the Police Superintendants Association noted in evidence to the Commons Home Affairs Committee:

> "Unfortunately, at a time when public finance is under considerable pressure, social investments which may not appear to have immediate, direct benefit, such as the long term prevention of juvenile delinquency, can become targets for short term savings."[20]

Families and schools

Some of the most optimistic evidence in this report concerns the way that families and the education system can work together to reduce the risk of school failure – and thereby reduce the danger that children will be attracted to delinquent peer groups and criminal activities. The well-evaluated example of the Perry Pre-School Programme in the United States has translated theory into practice by suggesting that nursery education of a high standard can yield an impressive list of long-lasting benefits for disadvantaged children, including less involvement in crime.

It might reasonably be argued that identifying a crime prevention benefit among the many advantages of pre-school is merely gilding a case for under-fives provision which should already be unanswerable. Research in Britain suggests convincingly that the best, most stimulating pre-school experiences – whether delivered through a good play group or more formal nursery class – give children an educational head start.[21] The gap that most immediately needs bridging is, therefore, between those who have some worthwhile pre-school experience and those who have none.

The evidence from America is, however, quite specific in linking delinquency prevention benefits to a curriculum promoting child-initiated learning, so that children learn to make their own decisions and think ahead.[22] It is, therefore, encouraging that the Home Office has recently funded four experimental nursery classes in Lewisham, Liverpool, Manchester and Newcastle-upon-Tyne to be run by High/Scope UK, an offshoot of the educational foundation responsible for the Perry Pre-School research.[23]

The quality of pre-school provision is clearly germane to its success, but discussions about the curriculum content should not obscure the more fundamental problem over inadequacy of provision. It is 20 years since Margaret Thatcher, as Education Secretary, published a White Paper intended as the precursor of universal pre-school education funded by the state.[24] Not only has that policy never been enacted, but there is depressing evidence that those local authorities that have used their discretion to provide good nursery education are under increasing pressure from government spending restrictions to make cuts.[25] Given the cost-effective power of pre-school to improve children's attainment and behaviour in the years of compulsory education, this report has no hesitation in adding its support to the cause of universal provision. If this cannot be achieved, action should be taken to ensure the availability of publicly supported pre-school programmes of a high quality in socially disadvantaged neighbourhoods.

Indications on both sides of the Atlantic that cognitive and other gains from pre-school experience can "fade out" emphasises the need for continuing intellectual stimulation and high standards once children move into primary school. Chapter 4 set out the case for "effective" schools whose methods allow them to exert a positive influence over truancy and disruptive behaviour as well as educational achievement. As children grow older, schools become one of the forces against the formation of delinquent peer groups – disaffected young people whose shared anti-social attitudes and sense of failure reinforces their willingness to break the law. They also have a crucial role to play in preventing bullying. Research has pinpointed factors like the quality of leadership provided by head teachers, the consistency of approach by staff, the overall climate of the school and the extent to which children are challenged to give of their best – suggesting that the first aim of policy should be to replicate practice in the best schools among the worst. The knowledge gained from experiments in helping pupils with poor reading and mathematical skills, like the work in America of Dr James Comer, needs wider circulation and application.[26]

The ultimate effectiveness of pre-school and compulsory education may depend, however, on how far families are acknowledged as partners in the educative process. The advantage to children of having interested parents who reinforce and validate their learning experiences need not be doubted. Parental interest is one of the most powerful factors affecting children's progress in pre-school[27]. But it is also an obvious force for continuity of achievement through the transitions to primary and secondary schooling. Urie Bronfenbrenner concluded, in a review of Project Headstart and other pre-school interventions with children in America, that:

"The family is the most effective and economical system for fostering and sustaining the development of the child. The involvement of the child's family as an active participant is critical to the success of any intervention programme."[28]

Supporting families

Raising children is the most demanding yet potentially rewarding job that most human beings undertake. There are reasons, too, for supposing that just as family life has undergone major structural alterations in the 20th century, so the task of being a parent has become progressively more complicated and exacting. Observers, like the Netherlands criminologist Josine Junger-Tas,[29] have noted the declining influence of religion over family life. Social conventions that were once afforded the status of moral certainties – such as the dominant,

disciplinarian role of fathers as "head of the household" – have also fallen into disrepute. The status granted to the interests, views and individual rights of adolescents has made the traditional, authoritarian family an increasingly rare and anachronistic phenomenon. Instead, there has been the rise of "negotiating" households where parents no longer lay down a course of action for their children without attempting to seek their agreement. Television and video are, for better or worse, pervasive influences in the home with which previous generations of parents did not have to contend.

Parents are also expected to find their own solutions to the thoroughly modern dilemma that pits the desire to provide a better living standard for their children through paid work against the wish to stay at home with them, especially in their pre-school years. The dual-earner household is increasingly the norm.

Families are, meanwhile, more likely to experience divorce than any previous generation.[30] Partly as a result, parents are also more likely to be bringing children up on their own – with all that lone parent status implies about their relative poverty.[31] The help and experience that might once have been available to new parents from other family members living nearby has, meanwhile, been weakened by the dispersal of the extended family.[32]

Turning the clock back to moral and religious authoritarianism or to the "working father – stay at home mother" model of family life are no longer options, let alone solutions. In so far as compliance with the law has been eroded by a lack of moral certainty, the secular remedy must surely be to develop self-discipline and internal control in children together with their respect for, and personal stake in, the communities that they share. While exhortations for parents to act more responsibly may have their value, a more realistic and practical approach is to identify methods of supporting parents, especially those who are inexperienced and under grave stress.

The programmes described in Chapter 3 indicate the types of family support initiative that could yield dividends as part of an overall strategy to prevent delinquency. The fact that the projects selected for description concentrate on channelling assistance to parents of pre-adolescent children is entirely deliberate, since the first ten years are so clearly the period where parents' potential to influence long-term values and behaviour is at its peak. Attitudes and behaviour learned during early upbringing and schooling can be expected to influence children's later choice of friends in adolescence. But parents whose teenage children "get in

71

with the wrong crowd" may, by that stage, face uphill competition against peer group pressure. Organisations like Parent Network and Exploring Parenthood, as well as the Oregon Social Learning Center in the United States, have acknowledged that the parents of adolescents need special skills to successfully negotiate their children's potentially stormy transition to independence.[33]

They may also be confronted by actual offending – at which point the need to prevent further delinquency suddenly becomes acute. Ironically, far more attention, energy and money has been devoted to rehabilitative and diversionary work with young offenders than to primary prevention with families. Some approaches, notably Intermediate Treatment,[34] make a point of including parents as signatories to the contracts which young participants are required to sign. At a more extreme level, family therapy techniques are used at the Youth Treatment Service's St Charles Centre in Essex where juveniles found guilty of murder, rape and other very serious offences are detained.[35] It contributes to the major task of assisting families and the young people themselves in coming to terms with the enormity of what has occurred.

Other projects work by offering teenage offenders whose parental ties have broken down the support of a substitute "family". A pioneering fostering project run by National Children's Home and the Probation Service in Hampshire is an example.[36] Such interventions, alongside the community support work described in Chapter 5, are necessary if young offenders are to be diverted from the hugely expensive path that leads to recidivism and imprisonment. The focus of delinquency prevention in this paper nevertheless remains on whether families can be helped to secure the stable door before the horse has bolted.

The descriptive distinction which has been made between "universal" initiatives that would benefit any parent and those, of increasing intensity, which can be targeted on neighbourhoods and individuals is not particularly hard or fast. The different components of family support programmes are not easily compartmentalised: a specialist training programme for the parents of a behaviourally disturbed six-year old should, for example, include material which any family would find valuable. The structure adopted in Chapter 3 can, nevertheless, be broadly adhered to.

Parent education

The lack of any national plan for parent education remains as glaring an omission as it was when highlighted by Gillian Pugh and Erica De'Ath ten years ago.[37] Such a strategy should begin, as they suggest, by placing family planning and preparation for family life on the curriculum of every secondary school in the country. It would ensure that teenagers were made aware of the responsibilities of parenthood – and the special difficulties encountered by young single parents – as well as the means by which they can postpone child-rearing to a time of their own choosing.

The need thereafter is to build on the existing levels of care and advice given to pregnant women to ensure that they and their partners have access to continuing support – from professionals like Health Visitors and through contact with other young families – in their new role as parents. Reluctance to participate in parental skills education could be overcome, and greater understanding of child development stimulated, by a Government-endorsed parenting campaign, widely available videos and a national television series. Organisations like Parent Network and the information service provided by Exploring Parenthood could, meanwhile, be encouraged to expand their work. Evaluation of these and other projects would, hopefully, confirm their worth and identify directions for improvement.

The progress of doctors at the Maudsley Hospital in London[38] in introducing American parent-training techniques on video to the parents of behaviourally disturbed children should be monitored by policy makers as well as the medical profession. Given the strong statistical association between parental criminality and offending by their children, it is also common sense to expand the parent education programmes in prisons (See Preface) and the support given to prisoners' partners and wives.

Although reduced risks of delinquency are one of the looked-for consequences of improved parenting skills, the emphasis in any campaign should be on the positive aspects of raising a family and building parental confidence. As Gerald Patterson puts it:

> "I would simply explain to British parents that it is getting more difficult to raise children in our complex society and that all of us could do with learning new skills."[39]

Neighbourhood support

If it is thought that some support services are too specialised or expensive to provide on a universal basis, then neighbourhood centres may provide an effective compromise for targeting families at risk. It has clearly been demonstrated that when family centres open their doors to the whole community they have the ability to reach parents and children in difficulties without stigmatising them.[40] If their preventive work is to be extended to include delinquency, this is extremely important. Labelling children below the age of criminal responsibility as "potential offenders in need of treatment" would be practically as well as morally unjustified.[41] The best way to help the families of those children who appear to be most at risk is likely to be through a variety of services that are made relevant and attractive to them. Parent and toddler clubs, babysitting circles, health and fitness classes and a long list of other activities give parents respite and the chance to escape from social isolation. Once families are through the door, then the opportunity may be taken to interest them in more specialist help.

As Chapter 3 suggests, many of the services provided by neighbourhood projects are already relevant to crime prevention, ranging from play groups to family therapy. Their major objectives of strengthening families and preventing the need for children to be taken into care are at one with reducing the risks of delinquency. It would, therefore, be a retrograde step if such provision became the victim of cuts resulting from an increasingly narrow, cost-driven focus on crisis child protection work by local authorities.[42] As part of a delinquency prevention strategy their work needs to be reinforced and developed.

Family and group therapy are among the services which some centres already make available. Children with conduct disorders, those who truant and those who steal are likely to number among the presenting problems with which the therapist is faced. Evaluation and further research would, therefore, be especially helpful in this field to discover which of the many forms of therapy currently practised are most likely to prove effective in a crime prevention context. The experience gained by American practitioners who have made the treatment of aggressive, uncontrollable and delinquent children their special study, like those at the Oregon Social Learning Center, is already proving valuable in designing appropriate British initiatives.

Family preservation

There is evidence, however, that even in areas with an unusually liberal provision of neighbourhood centres, they will not reach more than a minority of the disadvantaged families[43] in their locality. This suggests a need for outreach work of a kind that encourages parents to make use of the services being provided. A parallel for this would be home visiting schemes, like that in East Moulsecoomb near Brighton described in Chapter 4, which have proved effective in persuading parents to take advantage of pre-school education.

Some families may be so beset by problems that

outreach must extend to the delivery of services in their own homes. The voluntary organisation Home-Start provides the example of a well-established model that has been replicated – sometimes under other names – in different parts of the country. Its value, described in Chapter 3, is that the help which volunteer parents provide, from tidying-up to practical advice on parenting, is made specially acceptable by being offered as an act of friendship. Families can be coaxed into coping without being made to feel inadequate or "de-skilled". The same, in the context of intensive support for parents of new-born babies at risk of abuse, is true of Newpin.

Intervention which can prevent the need for children registered "at risk" from being taken into care is not only desirable from the taxpayer's point of view, but is also in the long-term interests of preventing crime. Children who have been in care for long periods are found in disproportionate numbers in the population of Young Offender Institutions and prisons.[44] Conventional social work, armed with the 1989 Children Act, has a central part to play in this important task of keeping children out of care, although it does so under the pressure of increasing case loads and restricted budgets.[45] Once children are accepted into care there is also an improved understanding of how to minimise their stay, including efforts to maintain contacts with parents and to prepare families for their child's eventual return.[46]

At the eleventh hour, however, when parents know that the next step will be for the social services to seek a care order, the opportunity exists for more intensive home help than is currently available. Family aides, lacking formal qualifications, have had some success in preventing family breakdown, although their work is stressful and not well paid. Evaluation of the NCH Radford Shared Care Project in Nottingham suggests this is a potentially more effective model.[47] But attention should also be devoted to the practice of family preservation programmes, now widely adopted in the United States. The six-week commitment of trained professionals to individual homes has proved successful in keeping children out of care and appears to be highly cost-effective despite the intensity of work provided.[48] It deserves to be tested in Britain.

A strategy for preventing delinquency

A number of the most promising ingredients for inclusion in a campaign to prevent delinquency in the family belong equally in strategies to combat other social ills. Many of the existing initiatives described in this paper are, for instance, designed primarily to limit the number of children taken into care. But strategies to reduce the incidence of

73

children's psychiatric problems, to better their performance in school or to improve their quality of life in one parent families would also contain elements that overlapped.

This is not a sign of weakness in the case for delinquency prevention, but rather an impressive source of underlying strength. If the increasing human and financial costs of crime can convince society that preventing criminality is a desirable goal, then it is encouraging to know that action addressing the main risk factors will yield potential benefits in other spheres. If, on the other hand, the survival of valuable existing family support work is threatened by restricted funding for education, or social services, then it is in the public interest that its crime prevention potential should be better known and understood.

Models which have helped the present authors to suggest an outline strategy for social crime prevention have, variously, included a British programme for wider parent education,[49] a Canadian project for tackling children's emotional and behavioural problems,[50] overviews by Harvard University specialists of early childhood intervention programmes in the United States[51] and a U.S. Justice Department guide for communities combatting drug and alcohol abuse.[52] In summary, a family-based delinquency prevention programme might include the following ingredients:

Universal

- *Family planning and preparation for family life education in schools*

- *Ante and post-natal care, guiding new parents into networks of support and advice*

- *A national, mass-media campaign on parent education*

- *Access to parental skills training courses (publicly subsidised where necessary)*

- *Good quality, affordable childcare available for parents who choose to work*

- *Pre-school education of a high-quality, in partnership with parents*

- *"Effectiveness" programmes in primary and secondary school, ensuring minimum reading/mathematical skills and maintaining liaison with parents.*

- *Strategies to prevent bullying in schools.*

Neighbourhood

- *Open access family centres offering relevant services such as parent and toddler clubs; playgroups; toy libraries; parent training; money advice; after-school clubs; special group work (such as for victims of domestic violence, mothers who have been in care); family therapy.*

- *Remedial design work and improved management of high crime estates.*

- *Community policing, including preventive work with families.*

- *Clubs and holiday activities for children and young people.*

- *Participation of parents in the management of family centres, schools and other community projects.*

Home

- *Extension of health visits to the parents of young children as well as infants*

- *Befriending, babysitting and other outreach services – perhaps organised from neighbourhood family centres*

- *Family support volunteers, improving the ability of parents under stress to cope (such as Home-Start)*

- *Family preservation services, providing intensive support for families in the shadow of care proceedings (such as Newpin, Radford Shared Care Project and Michigan "Families First").*

One essential rider to the provision of all these services is that they be rigorously monitored and evaluated so that their effectiveness as a tool of social crime prevention can be improved. The paucity of research on promising project work in the United Kingdom means that some of the recommendations in this report have to be more tentative than firmer knowledge would allow. There are many aspects of the American experience of crime and its prevention that Britain would be ill-advised to follow, but an enthusiasm for evaluation and measuring value for money is not one of them. Experiments in social crime prevention are needed urgently, but their effectiveness must be rigorously monitored and assessed.

As a matter of common sense, delinquency prevention services must be made sensitive to the particular needs of ethnic and cultural minorities. One exceedingly large minority to which more attention should be devoted in terms of crime prevention is, however, men. This is not merely because men so heavily outnumber women as known offenders, but because the role of fathers in raising pro-social, responsible children has been unjustly neglected. Studies do not always agree about the relative influence of male and female parents over the children's resistance to delinquent behaviour, but the association which Home Office researchers found between delinquency and a lack of close feelings or understanding between teenagers and their fathers was significant in the case of both boys and girls.[53]

What is certain is that use of existing family support services that have a bearing on delinquency prevention is dominated by mothers. This partly reflects the prominence of lone mothers among the ranks of poor and disadvantaged families, but it is much more the consequence of a culture where the routine tasks of child-rearing still fall disproportionately on women.[54]

Gillian Pugh and Erica De'Ath expressed a view that: *"If shared parenthood were a reality and if men's roles as fathers were seen to be as important as their roles as workers, this might go some way towards giving parenting the value it deserves."*[55] Fathers may have become welcome partners in the labour suite from which they were once banished, but their emancipation as sharing, responsible parents is very far from complete. Researchers should end their discriminatory interest in the influence of mothers on children's behaviour and provide the information that is currently lacking on the parenting role of fathers at different stages in their children's development. A national parent education programme of the type recommended in this report should contribute to that process by making special efforts to target men.

Public policy

Preventing delinquency and crime by supporting families is good, sensible social policy. Its potential misfortune – demonstrated by ill-fated and poorly conceived strategies like the 1970s Community Development Programme (CDP) – is its location across the boundaries of different government departments.[56] Were a strategy of the kind advocated in this report to be adopted, should the lead responsibility fall to the Home Office (crime prevention), the Department of Health (children, health and personal social services), the Department for Education (schools), the Department of Employment (support for school childcare schemes through Training and Employment Councils), the Department of Social Security (poverty) or the Department of the Environment (local government, inner cities and housing)? Unfortunately, beyond stressing the need for departments to work together for a worthwhile and cost-effective cause, there is not a great deal more that can be said from the outside. However, just as government has not been slow to enlist – or even enforce[57] – the co-operation of parents in the fight against crime, so families should now feel entirely justified in demanding the full co-operation of government.

Prevention is better than cure and when public policy is wholeheartedly committed to the cause of prevention it can undoubtedly effect change. The reduction in drink-driving fatalities brought about over 15 years is one such example, and the drop in the number of peri-natal baby deaths is another. However, as David Farrington has suggested, comparison with the health services is instructive from another point of view:[58]

Each year vast sums are committed to researching the cause of different diseases and in support of experimental interventions designed to prevent them. If only comparable resources could be devoted to preventing the social cancer caused by crime, the savings in public health as well as wealth would surely more than justify the cost.

1 Home Office Standing Conference on Crime Prevention (1988)

2 ibid

3 Today newspaper. 6th December 1988

4 Michael, A. (1992)

5 Home Office Annual Report 1993 (CM 2208)

6 Mayhew, P. & Aye Maung, N. (1992)

7 Barclay, G. et al (1993)

8 Nearly half all known offenders are aged under 21. See Chapter 1

9 Hirschi, T. (1969)

10 See, for example, Rutter, M. & Giller, H. (1983) and Larzelere, R.E. & Patterson, G.R. (1990)

11 West, D.J. (1982)

12 Murray, C.(1990)

13 See Heath, A. (1992)

14 Utting, D. article in The Guardian (9th October 1991)

15 See, for example, West,D.J. (1982) and Kolvin, I. et al (1990)

16 Milton S.Eisenhower Foundation (1990)

17 Farrington, D.P. & West, D.J. (1990)

18 Burghes, L. (1993a)

19 Pugh, G. & De'Ath, E. (1984)

20 Association of Chief Police Officers / Police Superintendants' Association (1993)

21 Osborn, A.F. & Millbank, J.E. (1987)

22 Schweinhart, L.J. (1987)

23 Family Violence and Crime Reduction Projects funded by the Home Office Programme Development Unit. Commons Written Answer 26th June 1992

75

24 Dept.of Education and Science (1972)

25 See, for example, report in *Co-ordinate* magazine, March 1993

26 Cauce, A.M. ,Comer, J.P. & Schwartz, D. (1987); Comer, J.P. (1980a) and (1980b)

27 See Osborn, A.F. & Millbank, J.E. (1987); Schweinhart, L.J. (1987)

28 Bronfenbrenner, U. (1976)

29 Junger-Tas, J. (1993)

30 Kiernan, K. & Wicks, M. (1990) .Haskey, J. (1988) and (1991)

31 Burghes, L (1993a)

32 Willmott, P. (1986)

33 Sokolov, I. & Hutton, D. (1988) and Patterson, G.R. & Forgatch, M. (1987) and (1989)

34 See Curtis, S. (1989) for an overview

35 Their offences are those that would carry a prison sentence of 14 or more years in an adult court

36 Young Offender Community Support Scheme, Fareham, Hampshire. See also Milton, S. Eisenhower Foundation (1990) for an account of the Philadelphia "House of Umoja" project, offering young, black Americans a family "substitute". See also Reid, J.B (1992) for description of Oregon Social Learning Center's scheme for supporting foster parents caring for adolescents referred by the courts.

37 Pugh, D. & De'Ath, E. (1984)

38 See Chapter 3

39 Interview with Utting

40 Holman, B. (1988) and Gibbons, J. et al (1990)

41 See Chapter 3 for discussion of the strength of statistical "indicators"

42 See Holman, B. (1992b) for description of the problem

43 Gibbons, J. et al (1990)

44 See Home Ofice Research Department (1991) and Little, M. (1990)

45 See, for example, Gibbons, J. et al (1990)

46 See Millham, S. et al (1986) and Millham, S. et al (1993)

47 See Chapter 3

48 Kelly, S (1992)

49 Pugh, G. & De'Ath, E. (1984)

50 Ministry of Community and Social Services, Ontario (1990)

51 Weiss, H. & Halpern, R. (1988) and Halpern. R. & Weiss, H. (1988)

52 Catalano, R.F. et al (1991)

53 Riley, D. & Shaw, M. (1985)

54 Kiernan, K. (1992)

55 Pugh, G. & De'Ath, E. (1984)

56 For a description of CDP and other initiatives see Higgins, J. et al (1983)

57 See Chapter 6

58 Farrington, D.P. (1992)

Bibliography

Ainley, M. (1984) *Family Therapy in Probation Practice* in A.Treacher & J.Carpenter (eds) *Using Family Therapy: a guide for practitioners in different professional settings.* Basil Blackwell

Anderson, S.; Kinsey, R.; Loader, I. & Smith, C. (1992) *"Cautionary Tales". A Study of Young People and Crime in Edinburgh.* Centre for Criminology, University of Edinburgh

Association of Chief Police Officers of England Wales & Northern Ireland / Superintendants' Association of Endland and Wales (1993) *Written Evidence to the Home Affairs Committee Inquiry into Juvenile Crime.*

Bank, L; Patterson, G.R. & Rcid, J.B. (1987) *Delinquency Prevention Through Training Parents in Family Management.* The Behavior Analyst 10, pp.75-82

Banks, C.; Maloney, E. & Willcock, H.D. (1975) *Public Attitudes to Crime and the Penal System.* British Journal of Criminology,15pp.228-240

Barclay, G.C. et al (1993). *Digest 2: Information on the Criminal Justice System in England and Wales,* Home Office Research and Statistics Department

Barthel, J. (1991) *For Children's Sake: the promise of family preservation.* J. Edna McConnel Clark Foundation/Winchell (New York)

Bavolek, J.S. (1984) *An Innovated Program for Reducing Abusive Parent-Child Interactions.* Child Resource World Review, 2,pp.6-24

Bavolek, J.S. & Comstock, C.M. (1983) *Nurturing Program for Parents and Children 4-12 Years.* Family Development Resources Inc. (Eau Claire, Wisconsin)

Bebbington, A. & Miles, J. (1989) *The Background of Children Who Enter Local Authority Care.* British Journal of Social Work 19, pp.349-368

Bennum, I. (1988) *Systems Theory and Family Therapy* in E.Street & W.Dryden (eds) Family Therapy in Britain. Open University Press

Berrueta-Clement; Schweinhart, L.J.; Barnett, W.S.; Epstein, A.S. & Weikart, D.P. (1984) *Changed Lives. The Effects of the Perry Pre-School Program Through Age 19.* High/Scope Educational Research Foundation, Ypsilanti, Michigan.

Besharov, D. (1987) *Giving the Juvenile Court a PreSchool Education* in J.Q. Wilson & G.C. Loury (eds) *From Children to Citizens Vol III: Families, Schools and Delinquency Prevention.* Springer-Verlag (New York)

Bradshaw, J. & Millar J. (1991) *Lone Parent Families in the UK.* HMSO

Bright, J. (1992) *Crime Prevention in America - A British Perspective.* University of Illinois at Chicago: Office of International Criminal Justice.

Bowlby, J.H. (1951) *Maternal Care and Mental Health.* World Health Organisation Bulletin 3 (Geneva)

Bronfenbrenner, U. (1976) *Is Early Intervention Effective? Facts and Principles of Early Intervention: a summary* in A.M. **Clarke & A.D.B. Clarke** (eds) *Early Experience, Myth and Evidence.* Open Books pp.247-256.

Burghes, L. (1993a) *One Parent Families: Policy Options for the 1990s.* Family Policy Studies Centre / Joseph Rowntree Foundation

Burghes, L (1993b) *Lone Parenthood and Family Disruption: the outcomes for children.* Family Policy Studies Centre (forthcoming)

Caddle, D. (1991). *Parenthood Training for Young Offenders: an evaluation of courses in Young Offender Institutions.* Home Office Research and Planning Unit Paper 63.

Campbell, A. (1981) *Girl Delinquents.* Basil Blackwell.

Capaldi, D.M. & Patterson, G.R. (1991) *Relation of Parental Transitions to Boys' Adjustment Problems: i. a linear hypothesis. ii. mothers at risk for transitions and unskilled parenting.* Developmental Psychology 27, No 3, pp.189 501

Cass, B. (1990) *Why Public Investment in Child Care Matters: Economic and Social Issues.* Lady Gowrie Child Centre

Catalano, R.F.; Chappell, P.T.; Hawkins, J.D.; Irvine S.M. & Resnick, H.M. (1991) *Communities That Care: Action for Drug Abuse Prevention: a guide for community leaders.* U.S. Department of Justice/ Jossey Bass

Cauce, A.M., Comer, J.P & Schwartz, D. (1987) *Long Term Effects of a Systems-Oriented School Prevention Programme.* American Journal of Orthopsychiatry. Vol. 57, pp.127-131

Cernkovich, S.A. & Giordano P.C. (1987) *Family Relationships.* Criminology 25, No 2, pp.295-321

Cherlin, A.J.; Furstenburg, F.F.jr.; Chase-Lansdale, P.L.; Kiernan, K.E.; Robins, P.K.; Ruane Morrison, D & Teitler, J.O. (1991) *Longitudinal Studies of Effects of Divorce on Children in Great Britain and the United States.* Science 252, 7th June 1991.

Clarke, R.V.G (ed) *Tackling Vandalism.* Home Office Research Study 47, HMSO.

Cohen, B (1990) *Caring for Children: report for the European Commission's Childcare Network on Childcare Services and Policy in the UK.* Scottish Child and Family Alliance / Family Policy Studies Centre.

Cohen, B. & Fraser, N. (1991) *Childcare in a Modern Welfare System. Social Policy.* Paper No 6, Institute for Public Policy Research

Coleman, A. (1987) *Utopia on Trial.* Hilary Rose

Comer,J.P. (1980a) *Improving the Quality and Continuity of Relationships in the Inner City Schools.* Journal of the American Academy of Child Psychiatry, 15, pp.535-545

Comer,J.P. (1980b) *School Power: Implications of an Intervention Project.* Free Press (New York).

Crellin, E.; Pringle, M.K. & West, P. (1971) *Born Illegitimate, a Report by the National Children's Bureau.* National Foundation for Educational Research

Crime Concern (1992) *Crime Reduction Programmes - a progress report*

Criminal Statistics, England and Wales (HMSO)

Currie, E. (1985) *Confronting Crime: an American challenge.* Pantheon/Random House (New York)

Curtis, S. (1989) *Juvenile Offending.* Batsford

Cyster, R. et al (1979) *Parental Involvement in Primary Schools.* NFER

Davie, R; Butler, N.R. & Goldstein, H. (1972) *From Birth to Seven: a report of the National Child Development Study.* Longmans

Davies, M. (1969) *Probationers in their Social Environment.* Home Office Research Study No 2. HMSO

Dawson, N. & McHugh, B. (1986) *Application of a Family Systems Approach in an Education Unit.* Maladjustment and Therapeutic Education 4, No 2, pp.48-54.

Dept. for Education (1992) *Exclusions: a discussion paper.*

Dept. of Education and Science (1972) *Education: A Framework for Expansion.* (White Paper) HMSO

Dept. of Education and Science(1989) *The Use of School Premises for Childcare Provision Out of School Hours.* Circular 16/10/89

Dept. of Education and Science / Welsh Office (1989) *Discipline in Schools.* Report of the Committee of Enquiry chaired by Lord Elton. HMSO

Dept. for Education / Welsh Office (1992) *Choice and Diversity; a new framework for schools.* White Paper. HMSO

Dept. of the Environment (1981) *Reducing Vandalism on Public Housing Estates.* HDD occasional paper 1/81. HMSO

Dept. of the Environment (1991) *A Handbook of Estate Improvement Vol 2, External Areas.* HMSO

Douglas, J.W.B. (1964) *The Home and The School.* MacGibbon and Kee

Douglas, J.W.B. (1968) *All Our Future.* Peter Davies

Egeland B. & Kreutzer T. (1991) *A Longitudinal Study of the Effects of Maternal Stress and Protective Factors on the Development of High-Risk Children* in E.M. Cummings, A.L. Greene & K.H. Karraker (eds) *Life-Span Developmental Psychology: perspectives on stress and coping.* Lawrence Erlbaum Associates

Emery, R.E. (1982) *Interparental Conflict and the Children of Discord and Divorce.* Psychological Bulletin 92 pp.310-330

Elliott, D.S. & Huizinga, D. (1983) *Social Class and Delinquent Behavior in a NatIonal Youth Panel.* Criminology 21, No 2, pp.149-177

Erickson, M.F.; Sroufe, L.A. & Egeland, B. (1985) *The Relationship Between Quality of Attachment and Behavior Problems in Preschool in a High-Risk Sample* in I. Bretherton and E. Waters (eds) *Growing Points of Attachment Theory and Research.* Monographs of The Society for Research in Child Development, Serial No 209, Vol 50 Nos 1-2, pp.147-166

Falloon, I.R.H. (1988) *Behavioural Family Therapy: systems, structures and strategies* in E.Street & W.Dryden (eds) *Family Therapy in Britain.* Open University Press

Family Policy Studies Centre (1991) . Family Finances: Fact Sheet No 4.

Family Expenditure Survey. (HMSO).

Farrington, D.P. (1979) *Longitudinal Research on Crime and Delinquency* in N.Morris & M.Tonry (eds) *Crime and Justice: an annual review of research Vol 1,* pp.289-348. University of Chicago Press.

Farrington, D.P. (1999) *Implications of Criminal Career Research for the Prevention of Offending .* Journal of Adolescence,13, pp.93-113

Farrington, D.P. (1992a) Trends in English Juvenile Delinquency and their Explanation. International Journal of Comparative and Applied Criminal Justice, 16, No2, pp.151-163

Farrington, D.P. (1992b) *Editorial* in Criminal Behavior and Mental Health, 2, pp.iii-v

Farrington, D.P. (1993) *Understanding and Preventing Bullying* in M.Tonry (ed) Crime and Justice, Vol.17. University of Chicago Press (forthcoming)

Farrington, D.P. et al (1986) *Understanding and Controlling Crime - Towards a New Research Strategy.* Springer Verlag, New York

Farrington, D.P & West, D.J. (1990) *The Cambridge Study in Delinquent Development: a long-term follow-up of 411 London males* in G. Kaiser, & H-J. Kerner (eds), *Criminality: Personality, Behaviour, Life History.* Springer-Verlag (Berlin)

Ferri, E. (1976) *Growing-Up in a One Parent Family.*National Foundation for Educational Research.

Field, S. (1990). *Trends in Crime and their Interpretation: a study of recorded crime in post-war England and Wales.* Home Office Research Study 119. HMSO

Finch, J. (1984) *A First Class Environment? Working Class Playgroups as PreSchool Experience* British Education Research Journal 10.1. pp.3-17

Fleming, J. & Ward, D. (1992)*"For the Children to be Alright, the Mothers need to be Alright" An Alternative to Removing the Child: the Radford Shared Care Project.* Centre for Social Action, Nottingham University / National Children's Home.

Forehand, R.L. & McMahon, R.J. (1981) *Helping the Noncompliant Child: a clinician's guide to parent training.* Guilford Press (New York)

Fox Harding, L. (1991) *Perspectives in Child Care Policy.* Longman

Fraser, W.F.; Hawkins, J.D. & Howard, M.O. (1988) *Parent Training for Delinquency Prevention.* Child & Youth Services 11, No 1, pp.93-125

Gent, M. (1992) *Parenting Assessment: The Parent/ Child Game.* Nursing Standard, April 8, Vol.6, No.29 pp.31-35

Gibbons, J. & Thorpe, S. (1989) *Can Voluntary Support Projects Help Vulnerable Families? The Work of Home-Start.* British Journal of Social Work 19, pp.189-202

Gibbons, J. with Thorpe, S. & Wilkinson, P. (1990) *Family Support & Prevention..* National Institute for Social Work / HMSO

Gill, K. (1992) *Tackling Youth Crime - A Practical Guide.* Crime Concern

Gladstone, F. (1978) *Vandalism Among Adolescent Boys* in R.V.G Clarke (ed) *Tackling Vandalism*. Home Office Research Study 47, HMSO.

Glueck, S. & Glueck, E.T. (1950) *Unravelling Juvenile Delinquency*. Harvard University Press.

Gorrell-Barnes, G. (1984) *Working With Families*. British Association of Social Workers / Macmillan

Gove, W.R. & Crutchfield, R.D. (1982) *The Family and Juvenile Delinquency*. Sociological Quarterly 23, pp.301-319

Graham, J. (1988) *Schools, Disruptive Behaviour and Delinquency*. Home Office Research Study No 96. HMSO

Graham, J. (1989) Families, Parenting Skills and Delinquency. Home Office Research Bulletin.

Graham, J. (1990) *Crime Prevention Strategies in Europe and North America*. Paper No 18, Helsinki Institute for Crime Prevention and Control, affiliated with the United Nations

Graham, J. & Smith, D.I. (1993) *Diversion from Offending: the role of the Youth Service*. Crime Concern.

Halpern, R. & Weiss, H. (1988)*What is Known about the Effectiveness of Family Oriented Early Childhood Intervention Programs*. Unpublished paper from Harvard Family Research Project, Harvard University School of Education.

Hannon, P. et al (1991) *The Sheffield Early Literary Development Project*. Current issues in Early Childhood 44 (Cited in: Mortimore P. (1991) *Bucking the Trends: Promoting Successful Urban Education* Times Educational Supplement/Greenwich Annual Lecture.)

Hardiker, P.; Exton, K. & Barker, M. (1989) *Policies and Practices in Preventive Child Care*. Report to the Department of Health. Supplement II. School of Social Work, University of Leicester.

Hardiker, P.; Exton, K. & Barker,M. (1991a) *The Social Policy Contexts of Prevention in Child Care*. British Journal of Social Work, 21, pp.341-359

Hardiker, P.; Exton, K. & Barker, M. (1991b) *Policies and Practices in Preventive Child Care*. Avebury.

Haskey, J. (1988) *Trends in Marriage & Divorce, and cohort analyses of the proportions of marriages ending in divorce*. Population Trends 54, pp.21-28. HMSO.

Haskey, J. (1990) *The Children of Families Broken by Divorce*. Population Trends 61, pp.34-42. HMSO

Haskey, J. (1991) *Estimated Numbers and Demographic Characteristics of One-Parent Families in Great Britain*. Population Trends 65, pp.35-47. HMSO

Haskey,J. (1993) *Trends in the Numbers of One-Parent Families in Great Britain*. Population Trends 70. HMSO

Hawkins, J.D.; Catalano, R.F.jr. et al (1987) *Delinquency Prevention through Parent Training: results and issues from work in progress* in J.Q. Wilson & G.C. Loury (eds) *From Children to Citizens Vol III: Families, Schools and Delinquency Prevention*. Springer-Verlag (New York)

Hawkins, J.D.; Von Cleve, E. & Catalano, R.F.jr (1991) *Reducing Early Childhood Aggression: results of a primary prevention program*. Journal of the American Academy of Child and Adolescent Psychiatry 30, No 2, pp.208-217

Hayes, R. and Saunders, L. (1992) *Social Policy Issues Report* Prepared for Kent County Council. Unpublished.

Heath, A. (1992) *The Attitudes of the Underclass* in D.J. Smith (ed) *Understanding the Underclass*. Policy Studies Institute.

Her Majesty's Inspectorate of Schools (1987) *Education Observed No. 5 - Good Behaviour and Discipline in Schools*. Dept. of Education and Science.

Her Majesty's Inspectorate of Schools (1989) *Education Observed No.13 - Attendance at Schools*. Dept. of Education and Science.

Hetherington, E.M.; Cox, M. & Cox, R. (1978) *The Aftermath of Divorce* in J.H. Stevens jr & M. Mathews (eds) *Mother-Child, Father-Child Relations*. The National Association for the Education of Young Children (Washington D.C.)

Higgins, J.; Deakin, N.; Edwards, J.; Wicks, M. (1983) *Government & Urban Poverty: inside the policy making process*. Basil Blackwell

Hirschi, T. (1969) *Causes of Delinquency*. University of California Press.

Hirschi, T, Hindelang, M. & Weis, J. (1982) *Reply to Tittle et al* in American Sociological Review 47, No 3 p435 (quoted in E. Currie: *Confronting Crime*)

Holman, B. (1983) *Resourceful Friends*. Children's Society

Holman, B. (1988) *Putting Families First: prevention and child care*. Children's Society / Macmillan

Holman, B. (1992a) *Family Centres*. National Children's Bureau Highlight No 111.

Holman, B. (1992b) *Linking Up With the Locals*. Article in Community Care,30th July 1992

Holtermann, S. (1992) *Investing in Young Children: costing an education and day care service*. National Children's Bureau

Home Office Research and Statistics Department (1991) National Prison Survey. Research Study No.128

Home Office Research and Statistics Department (1993) *Notifiable Offences, England and Wales 1992*. Statistical Bulletin 9/93.

Home Office Standing Conference on Crime Prevention (1987) *Report of the Working Party on the Prevention of Juvenile Crime*. Home Office

Home Office Standing Conference on Crime Prevention (1988) *Report of the Working Party on the Costs of Crime*. Home Office

Home Office Statistical Department (1989).*Criminal and Custodial Careers of those Born in 1953, 1958 & 1963*. Statistical Bulletin No 32/89.

Jencks et al (1972) *Inequality: A Reassessment of the Effects of Family and Schooling in America*. Basic Books (New York)

Johnson, R.E. (1986) *Family Structure and Delinquency: general patterns and gender differences.* Criminology 24, No 1 pp.65-84

Jowett, S. et al (1991) *Building Bridges: Parental Involvement in Schools.* National Foundation for Educational Research

Jowett, S. and Sylva, K. (1986) *Does the Kind of PreSchool Matter?* Educational Research 28. No 1. pp.21-31.

Junger-Tas, J. (1988) *Causal Factors: Social Control Theory* in J. Junger-Tas & R.L. Block (eds) *Juvenile Delinquency in the Netherlands.* Kugler Publications (Amsterdam/New York)

Junger-Tas, J. (1993). *Changes in the Family and their Impact on Delinquency.* in *Criticial Issues in European Crime Policy.* European Journal on Criminal Policy and Research Vol 1, No1. Kugler Publications (Amsterdam/New York).

Kelly, S. (1992) in *Family, School and Community: towards a social crime prevention agenda.* Crime Concern.

Kempeneers, M. & Lelievre, E. (1992) *Work and the Family in the Twelve EC States.* Eurobarometer No 34. Eurostat. Luxemburg

Kiernan, K. (1992a) *The Impact of Family Disruption in Childhood on Transitions Made in Young Adult Life.* Population Studies 46

Kiernan, K.(1992b) *Men and Women at Work and at Home* in R. Jowell et al (eds) *British Social Attitudes: the 9th report.* SCPR / Dartmouth

Kiernan, K. & Wicks, M. (1990) *Family Change and Future Policy,* Family Policy Studies Centre / Joseph Rowntree Foundation

Kilbrandon Report (1964) *Children and Young Persons: Scotland.* Cmnd 2306. HMSO

Knight, B. & Osborn, S. (1992) *Supporting Families to Prevent Crime.* Home Office (awaiting publication)

Kolvin, I.; Miller F.J.W.; Scott, D.McI.; Gatzanis, S.R.M. and Fleeting, M. (1990) *Continuities of Deprivation?* ESRC/DHSS Studies in Deprivation and Disadvantage No 15, Avebury

Labour Force Survey *Quarterly results* published in Employment Gazette. Dept. of Employment

Larzelere, R.E. & Patterson, G.R. (1990) *Parental Management: mediator of the effect of socioeconomic status on early delinquency.* Criminology 28, No 2, pp.301-324

Laub, J.H. & Sampson, R.J. (1988) *Unravelling Families and Delinquency: a re-analysis of the Gluecks' data.* Criminology 26, No 3 pp.355-380

Layborn, A. (1986) *Traditional Working Class Parenting - an Undervalued System.* British Journal of Social Work 16, pp.625-644.

Lazar, I. and Darlington, R. (1982) *The Lasting Effects of Early Education. A Report From The Consortium of Longitudinal Studies.* Monograph of the Society for Research in Child Development 47.

Leeds Family Service Unit (1987) *Can Family Aides Prevent Admission to Care? An Evaluation.*

Lingard, A. and Allard, J. (1982) *Parent Teacher Relations in Secondary Schools.* Home and School Council

Little, M. (1990) *Young Men in Prison.* Dartmouth

Loeber, R.; Dishion, T.J. & Patterson, G.R. (1984) *Multiple Gating: a multistage assessment procedure for identifying youths at risk for delinquency.* Journal of Research in Crime and Delinquency 21, No1, pp.7-32

Loeber, R. & Dishion, T. (1983) *Early Predictors of Male Delinquency: a review.* Psychological Bulletin 94, No 1, pp.68-99

Loeber, R. & Stouthamer-Loeber, M. (1986) *Family Factors as Correlates and Predictors of Juvenile Conduct Problems and Delinquency* in M. Tonry & N. Morris (eds) *Crime and Justice - an annual review of research. Vol 7.* University of Chicago.

McCord, J. (1982) *A Longitudinal View of the Relationship between Paternal Absence and Crime.* in J. Gunn & D.P. Farrington (eds)*Abnormal Offenders, Delinquency and the Criminal Justice System,* pp.113-12. Wiley (New York)

McCord, J.; McCord, W. & Zola, I.K (1959) *Origins of Crime: a new evaluation of the Cambridge-Somerville study.* Columbia University Press (New York)

McGuire, J. and Richman, N. (1986) *The Prevalence of Behaviour Problems in Three Types of PreSchool Group.* Journal of Child Psychiatry 27 pp.455 -472

Mannheim, H. (1948) *Juvenile Delinquency in an English Middletown.* Kegan Paul.

Mayhew, P. & Aye Maung, N. (1992) *Surveying Crime: Findings from the 1992 British Crime Survey.* Home Office Research and Statistics Department Research Findings No 2.

Mednick, S.A; Gabrielli, W.F.jr. & Hutchings, B. (1984) *Genetic Influences in Criminal Convictions: evidence from an adoption cohort.* Science 224 pp.891-894

Michael, Alun (1992) *Study of the Financial Cost of Crime to Victims and the Whole Community.* Labour Party publication

Michigan Department of Social Services (1992) *Families First of Michigan* (booklet)

Millham, S.; Bullock, R; Hosie, K. & Haak, M. (1986) *Lost in Care: the problems of maintaining links between children in care and their families.* Gower.

Millham, S.; Bullock, R. & Little, M. (1993) *Going Home.* Dartmouth

Milton S. Eisenhower Foundation (1990) *Youth Investment and Community Reconstruction: a 10th anniversary report.*(Washington D.C.)

Ministry of Community and Social Services, Ontario (1990) *Better Beginnings, Better Futures: an integrated model of primary prevention of emotional and behavioural problems.* Queen's Printer for Ontario, Canada.

Minty, B. & Ashcroft, C. (1988) *Child Care and Adult Crime.* Manchester University Press

MORI (1989) Survey commissioned by Home Office

MORI (1993) Survey Commissioned by BBC TV "Panorama" 15th March 1993

80

Mortimore, P. (1991) *School Effectiveness Research: Which Way at the Crossroads?* School Effectiveness and School Improvement. Vol 2. No. 3 pp.216

Mortimore, P. and Mortimore, J. (1984) *Parents and School in Education* in Education 5, October 1984

Mortimore, P. et al (1988) *School Matters*. Wells: Open Books

Murray, C. (1990) *The Emerging Underclass*. Institute of Economic Affairs.

National Association for the Care and Resettlement of Offenders (NACRO) (1988) *Policing Housing Estates*. Report of a NACRO Working Group

National Association for the Care and Resettlement of Offenders (NACRO) (1991) *Preventing Youth Crime*. NACRO Juvenile Crime Committee

National Association for the Care and Resettlement of Offenders (NACRO) (1992) *Social Crime Prevention: the role of the family*. Briefing.

National Association for the Care and Resettlement of Offenders (NACRO) (1993) *Family Policy and Crime*. Unpublished briefing paper

National Children's Bureau (1990) *Statistics on Under Fives and PreSchool Services*

Nelson, D.W. (1991) *The Public Policy Implications of Family Preservation* in K. Wells & D.E. Biegel (eds) *Family Preservation Services*. Sage Publications (Newbury Park, California)

New, L. and David, M. (1985) *For the Children's Sake* . Strathclyde Regional Council Under Fives Final Report of the member/officer group. Penguin

Newman, O. (1980) *Community of Interest.* Anchor Press/Doubleday (New York).

Nye, F.I. (1958) *Family Relationships and Behaviour*. Chapman and Hall.

Office of Population, Censuses and Surveys (1990) *Marriage and Divorce Statistics 1837-1983*. Series FM2, No 16, HMSO

Olweus, D. (1979) *Stability of Aggressive Reaction Patterns in Males: a review*. Psychological Bulletin 86 pp.852-875

Olweus, D, (1984) *Development of Stable Aggressive Reaction Patters in Males* in R.J. Blanchard & D.C. Blanchard (eds) *Advances in the Study of Aggression Vol 1*. Academic Press

Olweus, D. (1990) *Bullying Among Schoolchildren* in K.Hurrelmann & F.Losel (eds) *Health Hazards in Adolescence*. De Gruyter (Berlin)

Olweus, D. (1991) *Bully/Victim Problems among Schoolchildren: basic facts and effects of a school-based intervention programme*, in D.J.Pepler & K. Rubin (eds) *The Development and Treatment of Childhood Aggression*. Erlbaum (Hillsdale, New Jersey)

Olweus, D. (1992) *Victimization by Peers: antecedants and long-term outcomes* in K.H. Rubin & J.B. Asendorf (eds) *Social Withdrawl, Inhibition and Shyness in Childhood*. Erlbaum (Hillsdale, New Jersey)

Open University Dept. of Community Education (1992) *Parents and Under 8s: a proposal to the Department of Health for a new Open University Community Education Course.*

Osborn, A.F.; Butler, N.R. & Morris, A.C. (1984) *The Social Life of Britain's Five-Year Olds: a report of the Child Health and Education Study*. Routledge & Kegan Paul.

Osborn, A.F. & Millbank, J.E. (1987) *The Effects of Early Education*. Clarendon.

Osborn, S. & West, D.J. (1978) *Effectiveness of Various Predictors of Criminal Careers*. Journal of Adolescence,1. pp.101-117

Page, D. (1993) *Building for Communities: a study of new housing association estates*. Joseph Rowntree Foundation.

Patterson, G.R. (1976) *Living With Children: new methods for parents and teachers*. Research Press (Champaign, Illinois)

Patterson, G.R. (1982a) *A Social Learning Approach Vol 3: Coercive Family Process*. Castalia Publishing Co. (Eugene, Oregon)

Patterson, G.R.; Chamberlain, P. & Reid, J.B. (1982b) *A Comparative Evaluation of a Parent Training Program*. Behavior Therapy 13 pp.638-650.

Patterson, G.R. & Forgatch, M. (1987) *Parents and Adolescents Living Together*. Castalia Publishing (Eugene, Oregon)

Patterson, G.R. & Narrett, C.M. (1990) *The Development of a Reliable and Valid Treatment Program for Aggressive Young Children*. International Journal of Mental Health 19, No 3, pp.19-26

Pilling, D. (1990) *Escape from Disadvantage*. Falmer Press

Power, A. (1986)T*he Priority Estates Project Guide to Local Management*. Priority Estates Project

Pringle, M.K. (1975) *The Needs of Children*. Hutchinson

Pugh, G. (1992) *An Equal Start for all our Children*. Times Educational Supplement/Greenwich Lecture

Pugh, G. & De'Ath, E. (1984) *The Needs of Parents: practice and policy in parent education*. National Children's Bureau / Macmillan.

Quinton, D. & Rutter, M. (1985a) *Family Pathology and Child Psychiatric Disorder: a four-year prospective study* in A.R. Nicol (ed) *Longitudinal Studies in Child Psychology and Psychiatry*. John Wiley & Sons Ltd.

Quinton, D. & Rutter, M. (1985b) Parenting Behaviour of Mothers Raised in Care in A.R. Nicol (ed) *Longitudinal Studies in Child Psychology and Psychiatry*. John Wiley & Sons Ltd.

Rankin, J.H. & Wells, L.E. (1987) *The Preventive Effect of the Family on Delinquency* in E.H. Johnson (ed) *Handbook on Crime and Delinquency Prevention*. Greenwood Press

Reay, R. (1988) *Structural Family Therapy* in E.Street & W.Dryden (eds) *Family Therapy in Britain*. Open University Press

Reid, J.B. (1992) *Involving Parents in the Prevention of Conduct Disorder: rationale, problems and tactics*. Community Psychologist

81

Renken, B.; Egeland, B.; Marvinney, D.; Mangelsdorf, S. and Sroufe, L.A. (1989) *Early Childhood Antecedents of Aggression and Passive-Withdrawal in Early Elementary School.* Journal of Personality 57, No 2 pp.257-281

Riley, D. and Shaw, M. (1985) *Parental Supervision and Juvenile Delinquency.* Home Office Research Study 83, HMSO.

Riley, D. (1987) note in British Journal of Criminology replying to Harriett Wilson. 27, No4.

Robins, L.N. (1966) *Deviant Children Grown Up .* Robert E. Krieger, New York

Roland, E. (1989) *Bullying: the Scandanavian research tradition* in D.Tattum & D. Lane (eds) *Bullying in Schools.* Trentham

Rutter, M. (1971) *Parent-Child Separation: psychological effects on the children.* Journal of Child Psychology and Psychiatry 12, pp.233-260

Rutter, M. et al (1979) *Fifteen Thousand Hours.* London: Open Books

Rutter, M. (1981) *Maternal Deprivation Re-Assessed.* Penguin

Rutter, M. (1985) *Family and School Influences: meanings, mechanisms and implications.* in A.R. Nichol (ed) *Longitudinal Studies in Child Psychology and Psychiatry.* John Wiley & Sons Ltd.

Rutter, M. & Garmezy, N. (1983) *Developmental Psychopathology* in E.M. Hetherington (ed), P.H. Mussen (series ed) *Handbook of Child Psychology, Vol 4, Social and Personality Development* pp.775-911. Wiley (New York)

Rutter, M. & Giller ,H. (1983) *Juvenile Delinquency: trends and perspectives.* Penguin

Rutter, M. & Madge, N. (1976) *Cycles of Disadvantage: a review of research.* Studies in Deprivation and Disadvantage No 1, Heinemann

Rutter, M.; Quinton, D. & Liddle, C. (1983) *Parenting in Two Generations: looking backwards and looking forwards* in N. Madge (ed) *Families At Risk.* Studies in Deprivation and disadvantage No 8, Heinemann.

Rutter, M.; Tizard, J. & Whitmore, K. (1970) Education, Health and Behaviour.Longman.

Schorr, L.B. with Schorr, D. (1988) *Within Our Reach: breaking the cycle of disadvantage.* Anchor Press/ Doubleday (New York)

Schweinhart, L.J. (1987) *Can Preschool Programs Help Prevent Delinquency?* in J.Q. Wilson & G.C. Loury (eds) *From Children to Citizens Vol III: Families, Schools and Delinquency Prevention.* Springer-Verlag (New York)

Schweinhart, L., Weikart, D. and Lerner, M. (1986) *Consequences of Three Pre-school Curriculum Models Through Age 15.* Early Education Research Quarterly, pp.15-45.

Schweinhart, L.J. & Weikart, D. (1993) *A Summary of Significant Benefits: the High/Scope Perry Preschool Study through Age 27.* High/Scope Press (Ypsilanti, Michigan)

Scottish Office (1993) Statistical Bulletins. *Recorded crime in Scotland 1992.* CrJ/1993/2

Shaw, M. (1986) *Are Parents Prepared to Be Responsible?* Home Office Research and Planning Unit Research Bulletin No.20. HMSO.

Sinclair, I. (1971) *Hostels for Probationers.* Home Office Research Study No 6. HMSO.

Skogan, W. (1990) *Disorder and Decline in American Cities.* Free Press

Smith, D. & Tomlinson, S. (1989) *The School Effect.* Policy Studies Institute.

Social Service Inspectorate (1988) *Family Centres: a change of name or a change of practice?* Department of Health.

Sokolov, I. & Hutton, D. (1988) *The Parents Book.* Thorsons Publishing Group

Sroufe, L.A. (1979) *The Coherence of Individual Development: early care, attachment and subsequent developmental issues.* American Psychologist 34 pp.834-841

Stradling, R., Saunders, L., and Weston P. (1992) *Differentiation in Action: a whole school approach for raising attainment.* National Foundation for Educational Research/Dept. of Education and Science

Street, E. & Dryden, W. (1988) *Family Therapy in Britain.* Open University Press

Sylva, K. (1988) *Does Early Intervention Work?* Archives of Disease in Childhood. 64, pp.1103-1104

Sylva, K. and Moss, P. (1992) *Learning Before School.* National Commission on Education. Briefing No.8.

Tittle, C., Villemez, W. & Smith, D. (1978) *The Myth of Social Class and Criminality.* American Sociological Review 43, No6, (quoted in E. Currie (1985) *Confronting Crime)*

Tittle, C. et al (1982) *One Step Forward, Two Steps Back: More on the Class/Criminality Controversy.* American Sociological Review 47, No 3, (quoted in E. Currie, 1985)

Tremblay, R.E.; McCord, J.; Boileau, H.; Charlebois, P.; Gagnon, C.; Le Blanc, M. & Larivee, S. (1991) *Can Disruptive Boys be Helped to become Competent?.* Psychiatry 54 pp.148-161

Tremblay, R.E.; Vitaro, F.; Bertrand, L.; Le Blanc, M.; Beauchesne, H.; Boileau, H & David, L. (1992) *Parent and Child Training to Prevent Early Onset of Delinquency: the Montreal longitudinal experimental study* in J.McCord and R.E. Tremblay (eds) *Preventing Antisocial Behaviour.* Guilford (New York)

Trojanowicz, R. and Bucqueroux, B. (1990) *Community Policing.* Anderson (Cincinnati)

Van der Eyken,W. (1982/1990) *Home-Start: a four-year evaluation.* Home-Start Consultancy, Leicester.

Van Voorhis, P., Cullen, F.T.; Mathers, R.A. & Chenoweth Garner, C. (1988) *The Impact of Family Structure & Quality on Delinquency: a comparative assessment of structural and functional factors.* Criminology 26, No 2.

Wadsworth, M. (1979) *The Roots of Delinquency.* Martin Robertson

Walters, G.D. & White, T.W. (1989) *Bad Genes or Bad Research?* Criminology 27, No 3, pp.455-485.

82

Warren, C. (1991) *The Potential for Parent Advocacy in Family Centres.* M Phil thesis, Southampton University; (quoted in Holman, B. 1992)

Watt, J. (1977) *Cooperation in PreSchool Education* (cited in Jowett and Sylva (1986).)

Webster-Stratton, C. (1984) *Randomized Trial of Two Parent-Training Programs for Families with Conduct-Disordered Children.* Journal of Consulting and Clinical Psychology Vol.54, No4, pp.666-678

Webster-Stratton, C. (1989a) *Systematic Comparison of Consumer Satisfaction of Three Cost-Effective Parent Training Programs for Conduct Problem Children.* Behavior Therapy 20, pp.103-115

Webster-Stratton, C. et al (1989b) *The Long-Term Effectiveness and Clinical Significance of Three Cost-Effective Parent Training Programs for Conduct Problem Children.* Journal of Consulting and Clinical Psychology 57,No4,pp.550-553.

Wedge, P. & Prosser, H. (1973) *Born to Fail?* Arrow Books

Weinraub, M. (1978) *Fatherhood: the myth of the second-class parent* in J.H. Stevens jr & M. Mathews (eds) *Mother-Child, Father-Child Relations.* The National Association for the Education of Young Children (Washington D.C.)

Weiss, H. & Halpern, R. (1988/1990) *Community-Based Family Support and Education Programes: Something Old or Something New?* National Center for Children in Poverty, Columbia University (New York)

Wells, L.E. & Rankin, J.H. (1991) *Families and Delinquency: a meta-analysis of the impact of broken homes.* Social Problems 38, No 1, pp.71-89

West, D.J. (1969) *Present Conduct and Future Delinquency.* Heinemann

West, D.J. (1982) *Delinquency: its roots, careers and prospects.* Heinemann

West, D.J. & Farrington, D.P. (1973) *Who Becomes Delinquent?* Heinemann

West, D.J. & Farrington, D.P. (1977) The Delinquent Way of Life. Heinemann

White, J.L.; Moffit, T.E.; Earls, F.E.; Robins, L. & Silva, P.A. (1990) *How Early Can We Tell? Predictors of Childhood Conduct Disorder and Adolescent Delinquency.* Criminology 28, No 4, pp.507-533

Wilmott, P. (1986) *Social Networks, Informal Care & Public Policy.* Policy Studies Institute Research Report No 655.

Wilson, H. (1975) *Juvenile Delinquency, Parental Criminality and Social Handicap.* British Journal of Criminology 15, pp.241-250

Wilson, H. (1980) *Parental Supervision: a neglected aspect of delinquency.* British Journal of Criminology 20, No 3, pp.203-235

Wilson, H. (1987) *Parental Supervision Re-Examined.* British Journal of Criminology 27, No 3, pp.275-301

Wilson, J.Q. (1983) *Raising Kids: How parents' mistakes produce brats and delinquents.* Article in The Atlantic, October 1983

Wilson, J.Q. & Herrnstein, R.J. (1985). *Crime and Human Nature.* Touchstone/Simon and Schuster (New York)

Woodhead, M. (1976) *Intervening in Disadvantage: a challenge for nursery education.* National Foundation for Educational Research

Woodhead, M. (1985) *Pre-School Education Has Long-Term Effects But Can They Be Generalised?* Oxford Review of Education 11, No2, pp.133-135

Wootton, B. (1959). *Social Science and Social Pathology.* Allen and Unwin

Young, J.C. & Hamilton, M.E. (1978) *Paternal Behavior: implications for childrearing practice* in J.H. Stevens jr & M. Mathews (eds) *Mother-Child, Father-Child Relations.* The National Association for the Education of Young Children (Washington D.C.)

Zigler, E. & Hall, N.W. (1987) *The Implications of Early Intervention Efforts for the Primary Prevention of Juvenile Delinquency* in J.Q. Wilson & G.C. Loury (eds) *From Children to Citizens Vol III: Families, Schools and Delinquency Prevention.* Springer-Verlag (New York)

The authors

Jon Bright is Director of Field Operations for Crime Concern, the national crime prevention organisation set up in 1988. He was previously the Coordinator of NACRO's Safe Neighbourhood Unit and pioneered multi-agency approaches to crime prevention and community safety on local authority housing estates. In 1990 he was awarded a Harkness Fellowship to study crime prevention in the USA. He has written widely on community safety and youth crime.

Clem Henricson is a freelance policy researcher and was formerly Head of Crime and Social Policy at NACRO. Prior to that she was crime prevention advisor to the Association of London Authorities and initiated the introduction of crime prevention powers for London boroughs. She has produced a number of publications on national and local crime prevention strategies.

David Utting is a freelance journalist and former Home Affairs Correspondent of the *Sunday Correspondent* and *Today* newspapers. He contributes on law, criminal justice issues and politics for *The Guardian* and *Independent on Sunday* and is the editor of *Family Policy Bulletin*. He has visited a number of social crime prevention programmes in the United States.

84